DOG SAYINGS

wit & wisdom from man's best friend

By Bradford G. Wheler

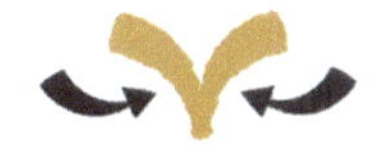

BookCollaborative.com
Cazenovia, New York

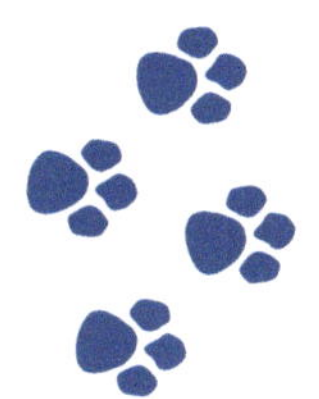

DOG SAYINGS

wit & wisdom from man's best friend

By Bradford G. Wheler

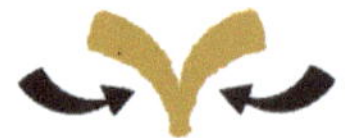

BookCollaborative.com
PO box 403
Cazenovia, NY 13035
BookCollaborative.com@gmail.com

ISBN-13 978-0-9822538-2-3

Library of Congress Control Number: 2010909672
Quotations, Art, Humor & Wit

PRINTER IN THE UNITED STATES OF AMERICA

Cover design by AuthorSupport.com
Interior design by Adina Cucicov, Flamingo Designs

Table of Contents

Introduction

I would like to thank everyone who participated in this project. In particular, I wanted to thank the artists and photographers who contributed their original works to this book.

It was exciting to check my email and find a wonderful range of new submissions from a wide variety of artists and photographers. The book features 49 artists from six different countries. They range in age from 9 to over 80. Many of the artists in this book are full time professional artists or photographers. Others love painting and photographing as a hobby. All are dog lovers.

I was very pleased to see how many of these artists are currently involved in animal rescue projects, giving generously of both their time and talent.

I established BookCollaborative.com to publish books based on the content provided by artists. The goal is to create a collaborative community to promote art in general. At the same time, artists have the opportunity to promote their own artwork in books. I also want it to be interesting and fun. I invite everyone to join us at www.BookCollaborative.com.

In selecting images for Dog Sayings, I tried to be inclusive. However, some artwork simply didn't fit the theme of this book. Other artwork did not make the cut due to various factors, such as missing the deadline, low image resolution, etc.

Printing color books with Lightening Source Inc's on demand system is about six times as expensive as printing black and white books. This factor limits the page count of a reasonably priced color book. It my hope that as technology progresses, the price for color on demand printing will come down. This would allow greater flexibility in the size of color books as well as the number of pages.

This book would not have been possibly without the help of many others. They include Adina Cucicov of Flamingo Design, who has done a beautiful job with the book's interior design, Marisa Cohen who not only wrote the artist biographies, and press releases, but also handled media placements, proofreading, and more, Nancy Kelner who turns my sloppy first drafts into a workable format, Hardy Capo who produces the wonderfully funny promotional videos featuring Todd and Matt, Stephanie Percells and Danial Brown of Parasane, who help with all things web related, and Simon and Ethan from the Apple store One to One training team who patiently keep teaching me. I would like to thank my lovely wife Julie for her support on this project and everything else. On a lighter note, I would like to thank Quincy our golden retriever for inspiring me to undertake "DOG SAYINGS; wit & wisdom from man's best friend".

I'm sure this book includes errors. For those I apologize.

Most of all I hope people enjoy "DOG SAYINGS; wit and wisdom from man's best friend." I believe it highlights man's love of dog and dog's love and devotion to man.

Bradford G. Wheler
Cazenovia, NY
October 2010

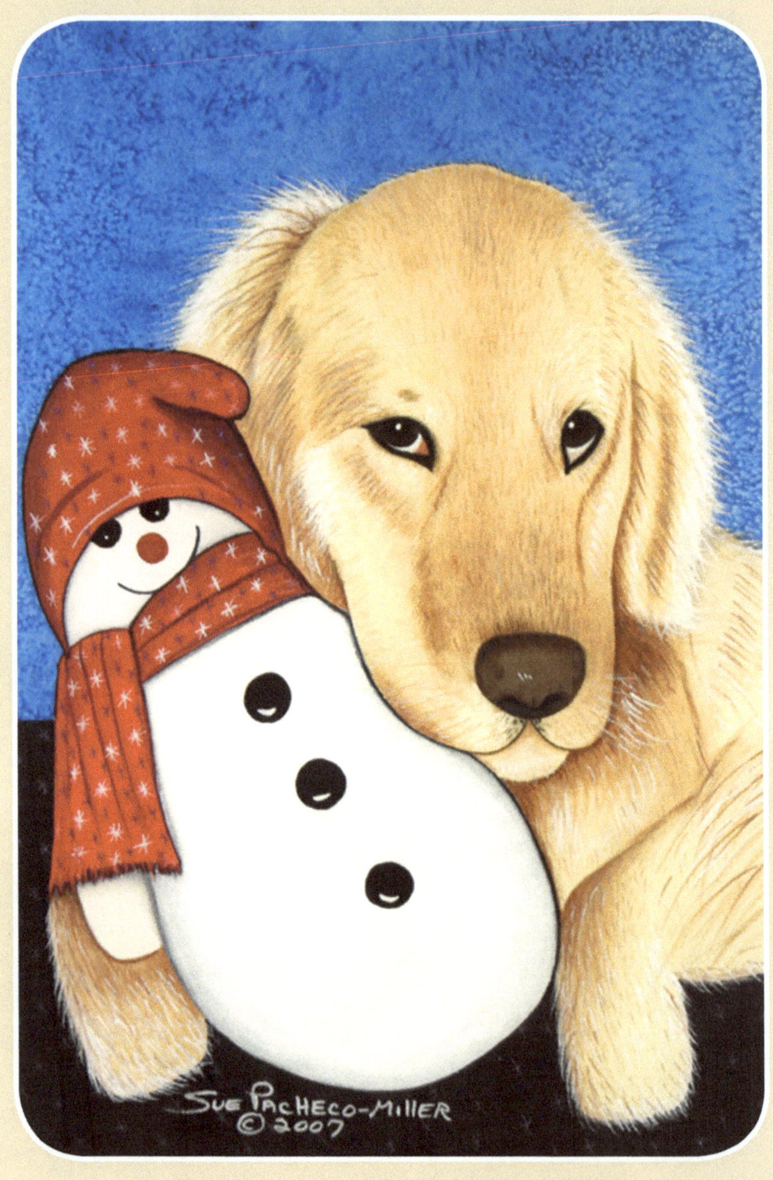

Sue Miller

Chapter 1

Love & Loyalty

Dogs are the most amazing creatures; they give unconditional love. For me they are the role model for being alive.

Gilda Radner, (1946-1989)

Dogs are our link to paradise. They don't know evil or jealousy or discontent.

Milan Kundero, (b. 1929)

Whoever said you can't buy happiness forgot about puppies.

Gene Hill, (1928-1997)

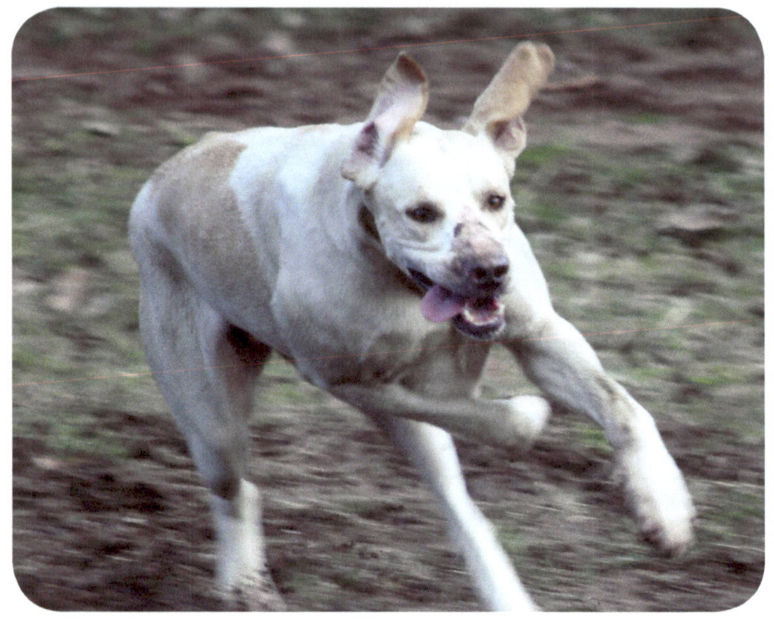

Kerry Ball

The poor dog, in life the firmest friend,
The first to welcome, foremost to defend.

Lord Byron, (1788-1824)

Man himself cannot express love and humility by external signs, so plainly as does a dog, when with dropping ears, hanging lips, flexuous body, and wagging tail, he meets his beloved master.

Charles Darwin, (1809-1882)

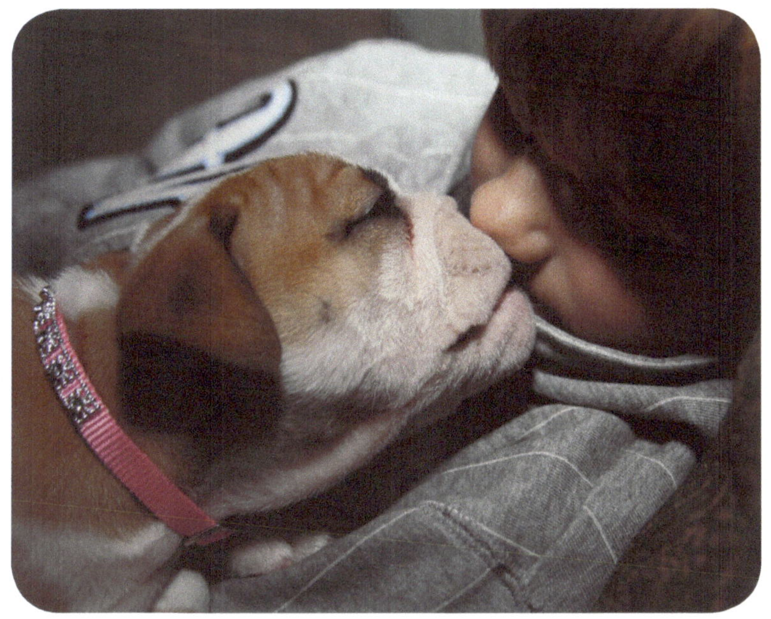

GENE GISSIN

There is no psychiatrist in the world like a puppy licking your face.

BERNARD WILLIAMS, (1929-2003)

Buy a pup and your money will buy love unflinching.

RUDYARD KIPLING, (1865-1936)

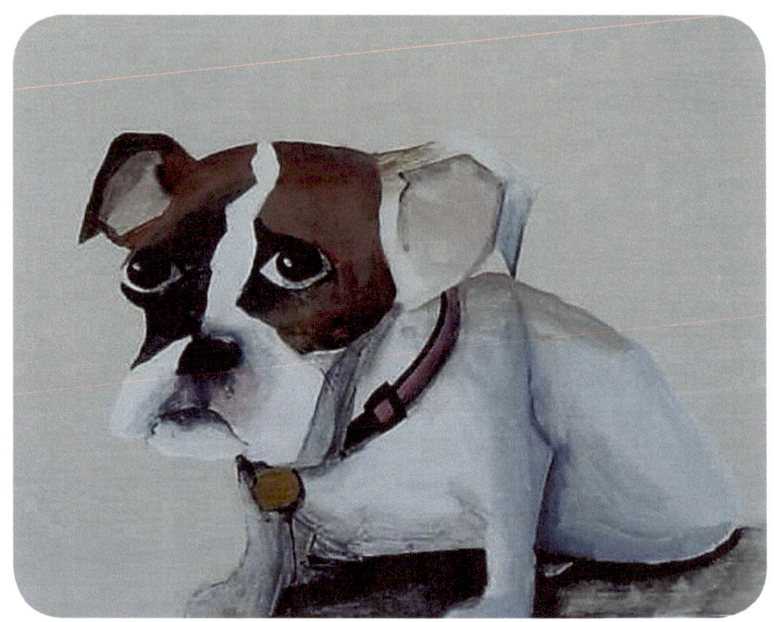

Tim Campbell

The greatest fear dogs know… is the fear that you will not come back when you go out the door without them.

Stanley Coren, (b. 1942)

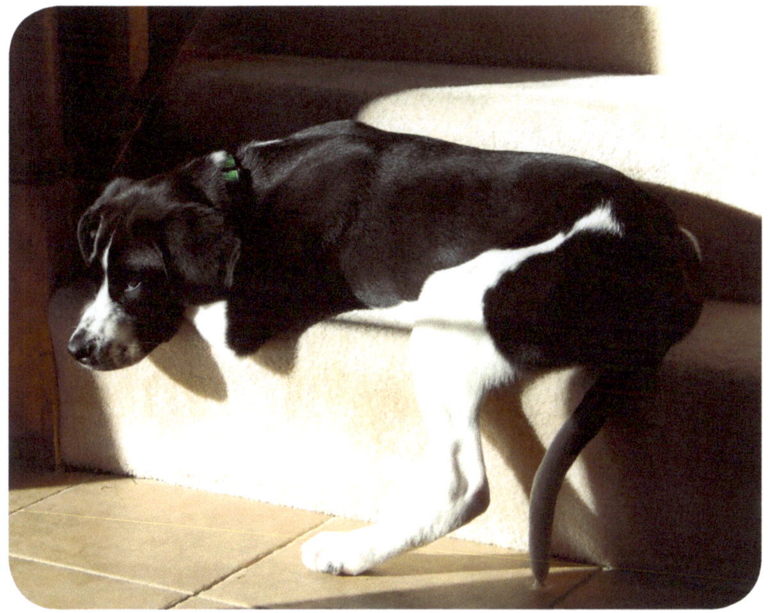

JESSICA PELSUE

His name is not wild dog anymore, but the first friend, because he will be our friend for always and always and always.

RUDYARD KIPLING, (1865-1936)

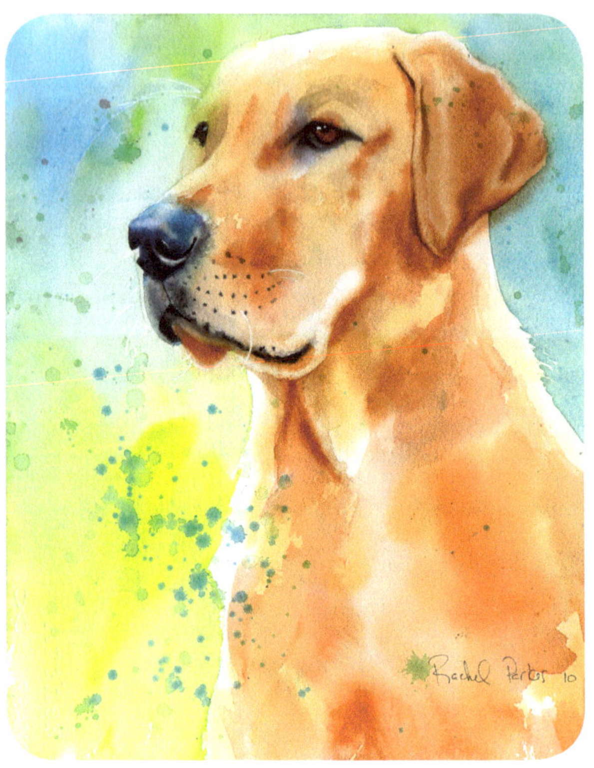

Rachel Parker

Dog! When we first met on the highway of life, we came from the two poles of creation… What can be the meaning of the obscure love for me that has sprung up in your heart?

Anatole France, (1844-1924)

CHAPTER 1

LOVE & LOYALTY

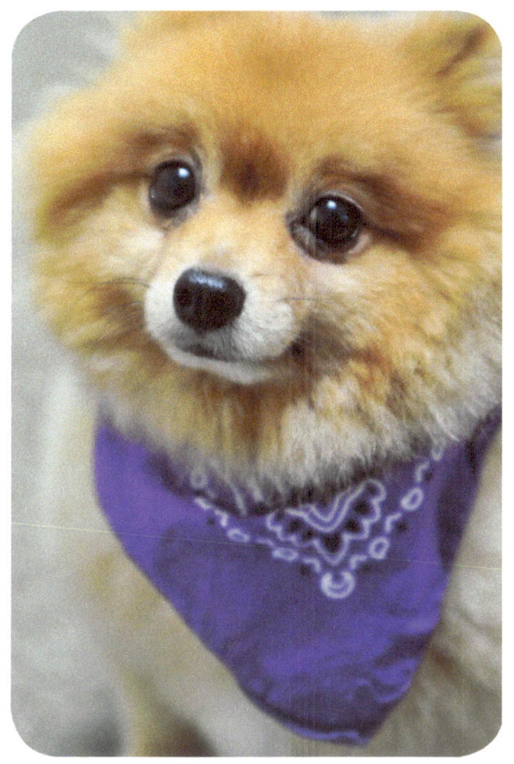

GABRIELLE UTZ

My little old dog;
A heart-beat At my feet.

EDITH WHARTON, (1862-1937)

Pray steal me not, I'm Mrs. Dingley's
Whose heart in this four-footed thing lies.

JONATHAN SWIFT, (1667-1745)

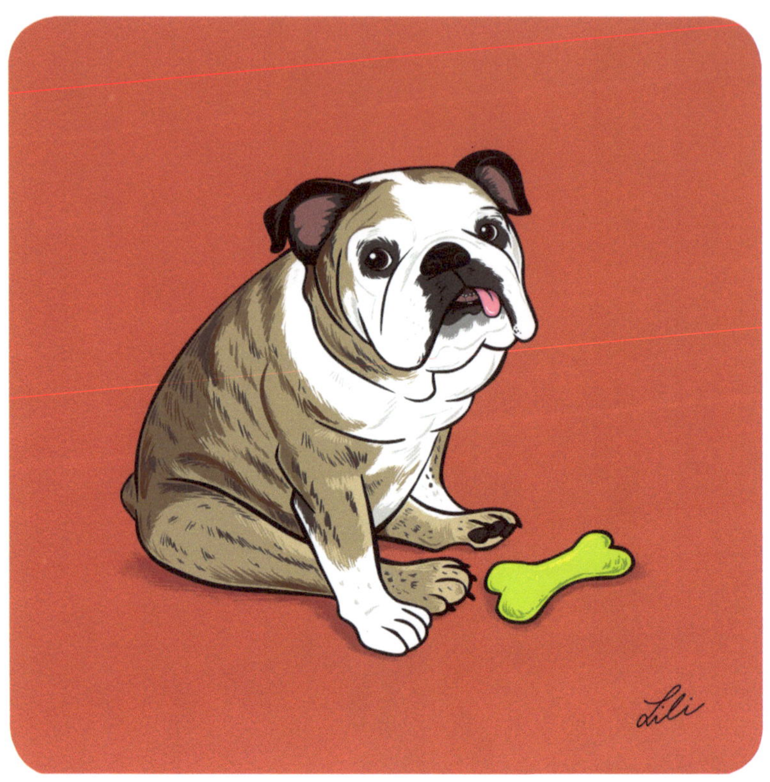

LILI CHIN

Happiness is a warm puppy.

CHARLES M. SCHULTZ, (1922-2000)

To err is human, to forgive canine.

PETER MAYLE, (B. 1939)

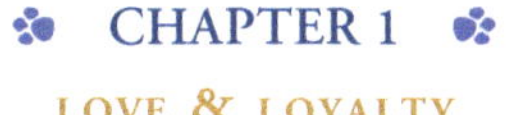

CHAPTER 1

LOVE & LOYALTY

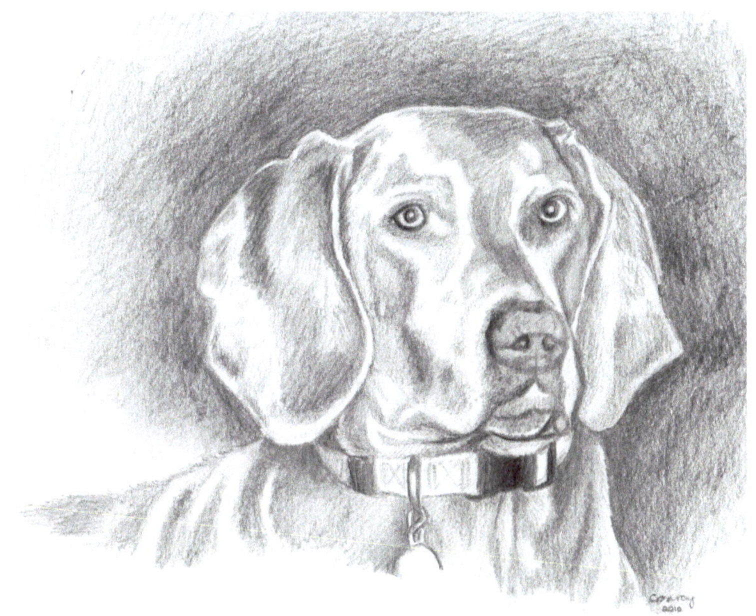

KATHERINE CONROY

The bond with a true dog is as lasting as the ties of this earth can ever be.

KONRAD A. LORENZ, (1903-1989)

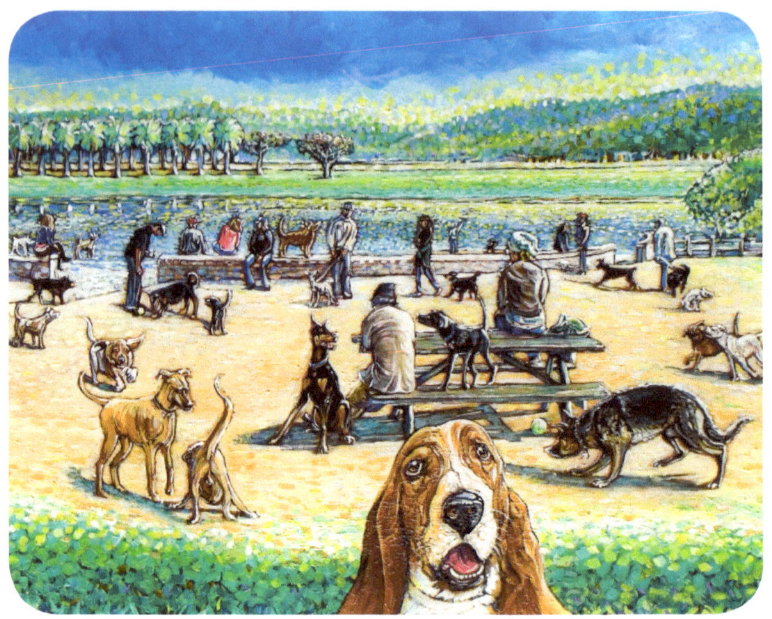

Kevin Rockwell

The great pleasure of a dog is that you may make a fool of yourself with him and not only will he not scold you, but he will make a fool of himself too.

Samuel Butler II, (1835-1902)

A puppy is but a dog, plus high spirits, and minus common sense.

Agnes Repplier, (1855-1950)

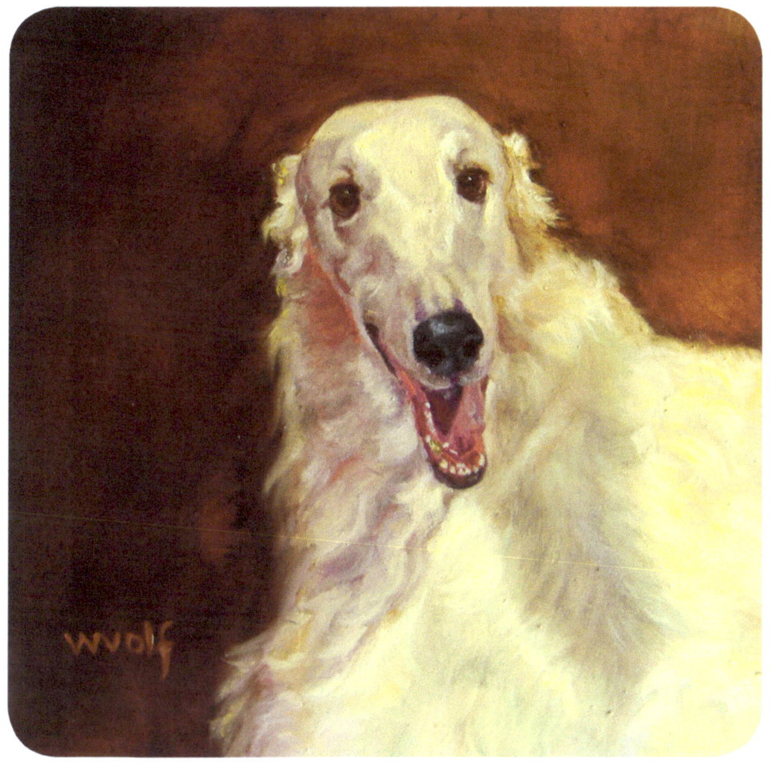

VALARIE WOLF

Old age means realizing you will never own all the dogs you wanted to.

JOE GORES, (B. 1931)

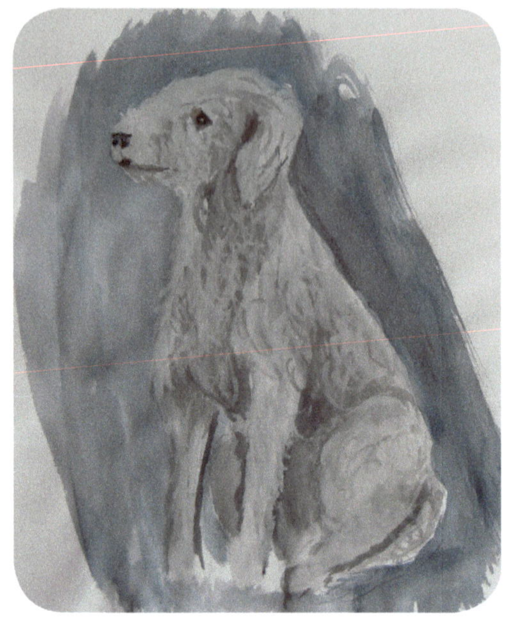

AMANDA HUGHES

Blessed is the person who has earned the love of an old dog.

SIDNEY JEANNE SEWARD, (B. 1922)

Old dog Tray's ever faithful;
Grief can not drive him away;
He is gentle, he is kind –
I shall never, never find
A better friend than old dog Tray!

STEPHEN C. FOSTER, (1826-1864)

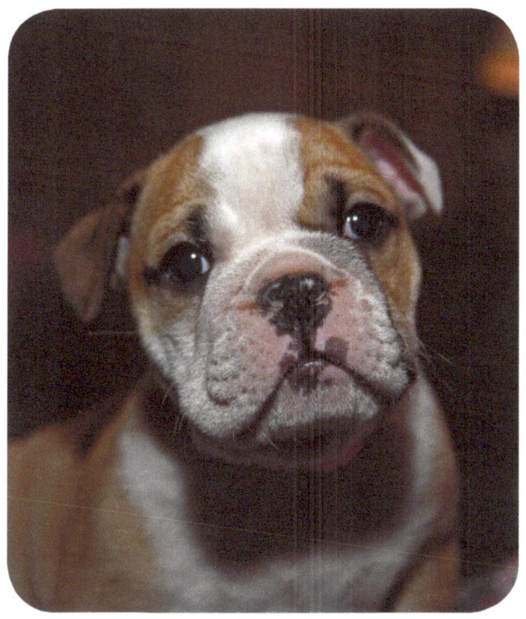

Gene Gissin

The most affectionate creature in the world is a wet dog.

Ambrose Bierce, (1842-1914)

The only creatures that are evolved enough to convey pure love are dogs and infants.

Johnny Depp, (b. 1963)

"Excavators digging through the volcanic ash that buried the ruins of Pompeii in A.D. 79 discovered a dog lying across a child. The dog, whose name was Delta, wore a collar that told how he had saved the life of his owner, Severinus, three times."

JOHN RICHARD STEPHENS, (B. 19??)

Until one has loved an animal, a part of one's soul remains unawakened.

ANATOLE FRANCE, (1844-1924)

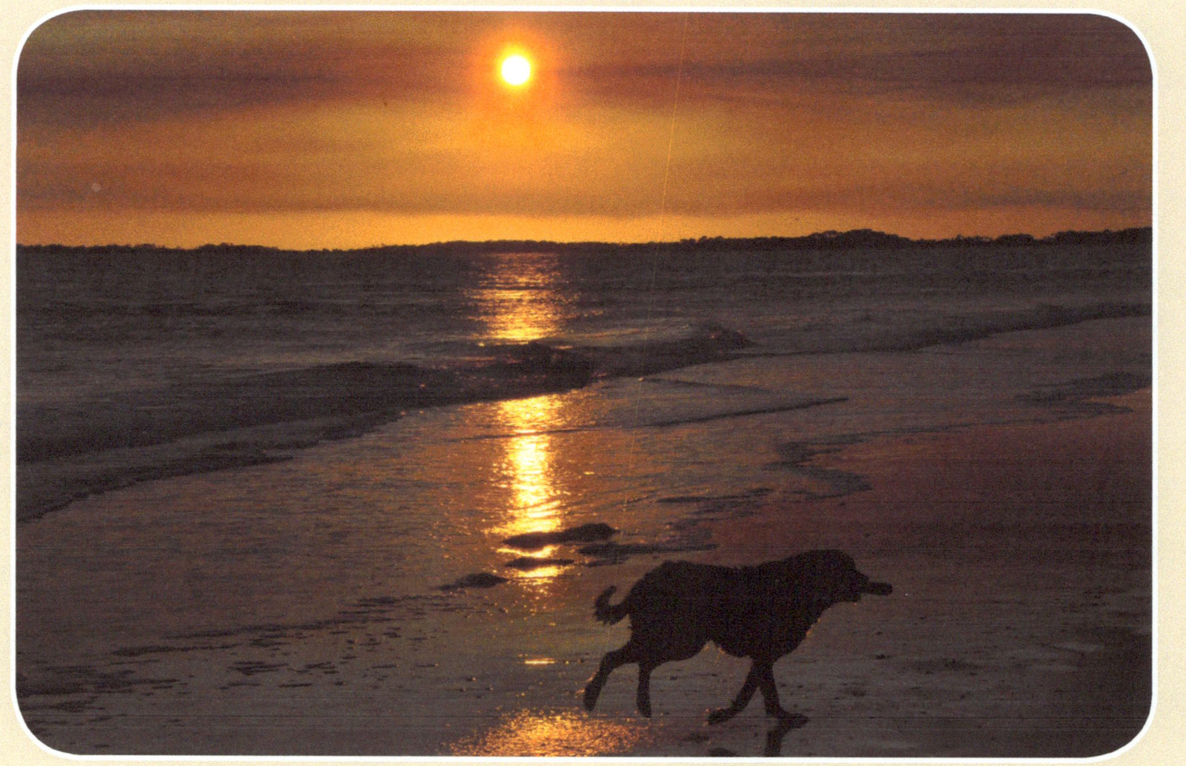

Too Fun To Quit

Charles Thompson

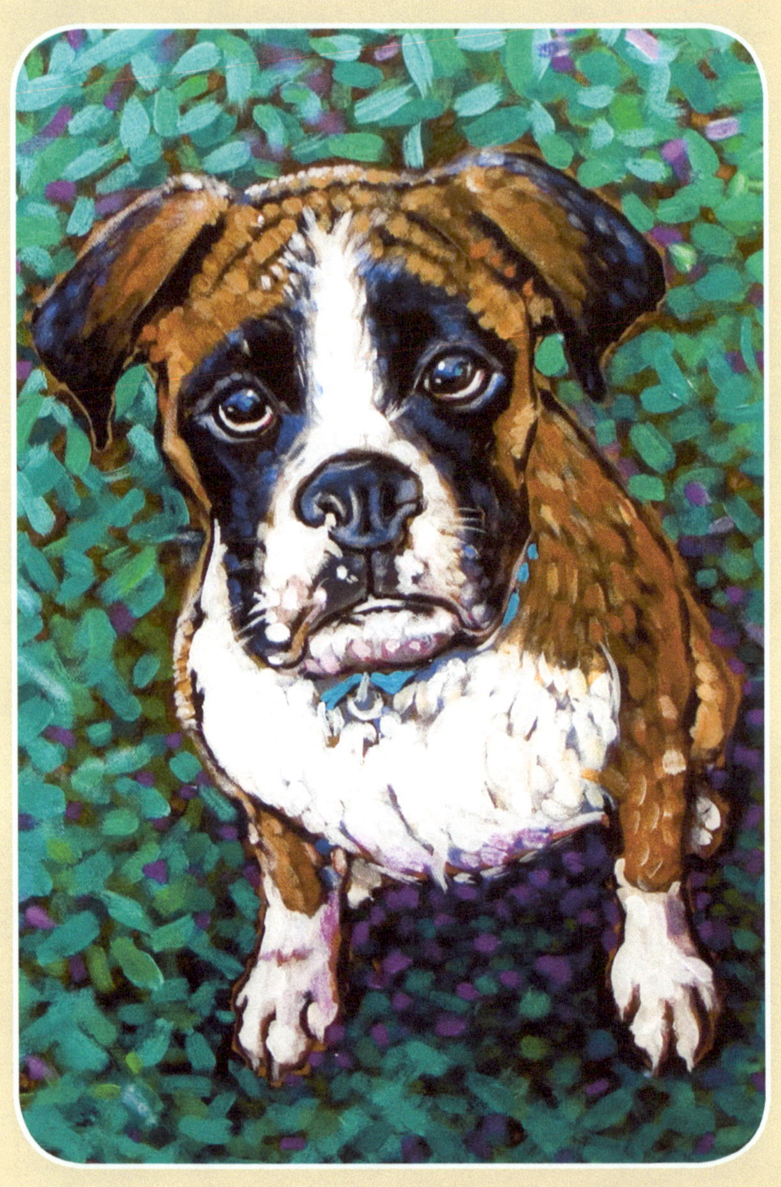

Kevin Rockwell

Chapter 2

Dogs & Politics

If you want a friend in Washington, get a dog.

Harry S. Truman, (1884-1972)

The greatness of a nation and its moral progress can be judged by the way its animals are treated.

Mohandas Gandhi, (1869-1948)

I love a dog. He does nothing for political reasons.

Will Rogers, (1879-1935)

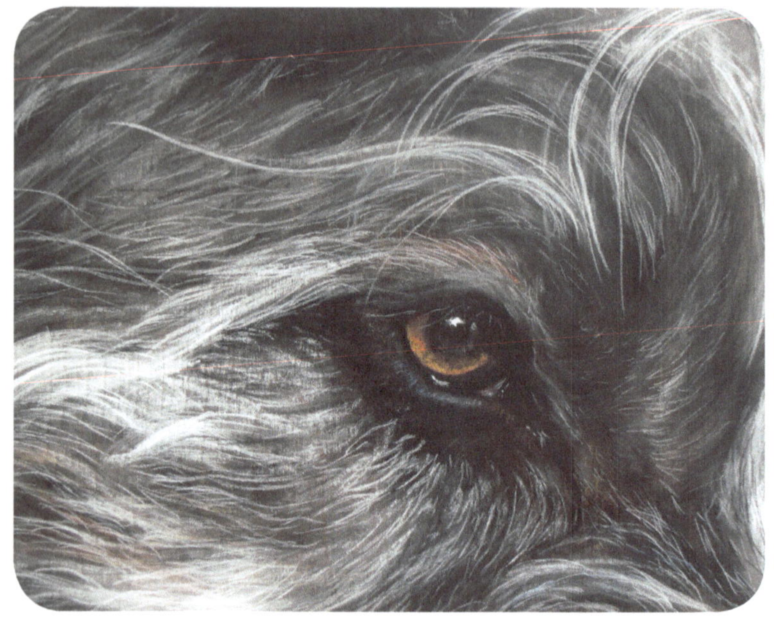

Kerry McGuire

Women, we might as well be dogs baying the moon as petitioners without the right to vote!

Susan B. Anthony, (1820-1906)

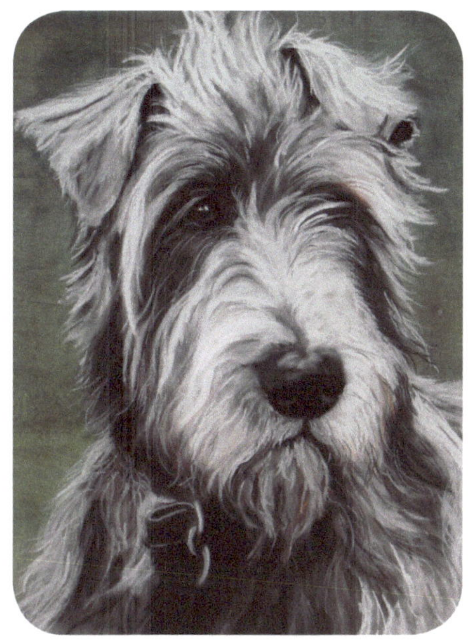

Killing the dog does not cure the bite.

ABRAHAM LINCOLN, (1809-1865)

KERRY MCGUIRE

Cute puppies and eternal glory. Add a splash of sex and you've got the essence of the American dream.

JACK BARTH, (B. 1946)

If only men could love each other like dogs, the world would be a paradise.

JAMES DOUGLAS, (1803-1877)

My dog can bark like a congressman, fetch like an aide, beg like a press secretary and play dead like a receptionist when the phone rings.

GERALD SOLOMON, (1930-2001)

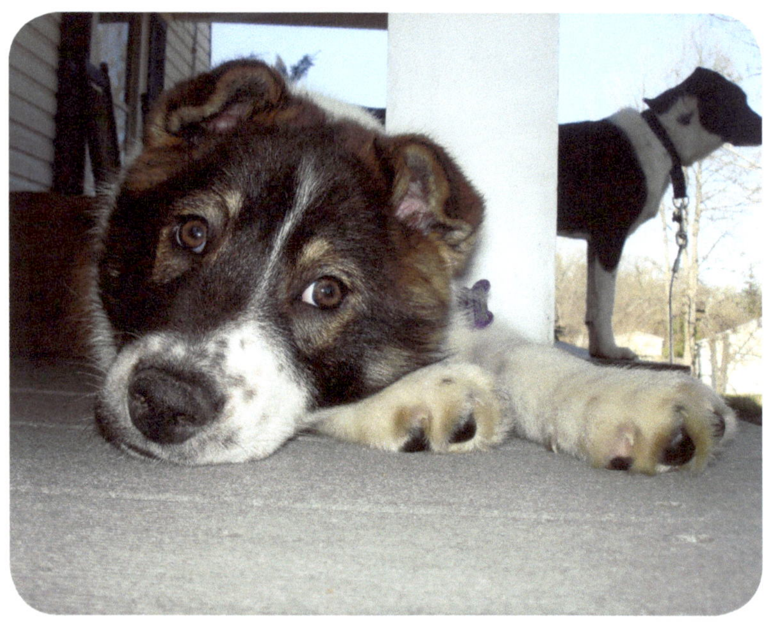

VICTORIA PATCHEN

The better I get to know men, the more I find myself loving dogs.

CHARLES DE GAULLE, (1890-1970)

Living with a dog is easy—like living with an idealist.

H. L. MENCKEN, (1880-1956)

To a man the greatest blessing is individual liberty; to a dog it is the last word in despair.

WILLIAM LYON PHELPS, (1865-1943)

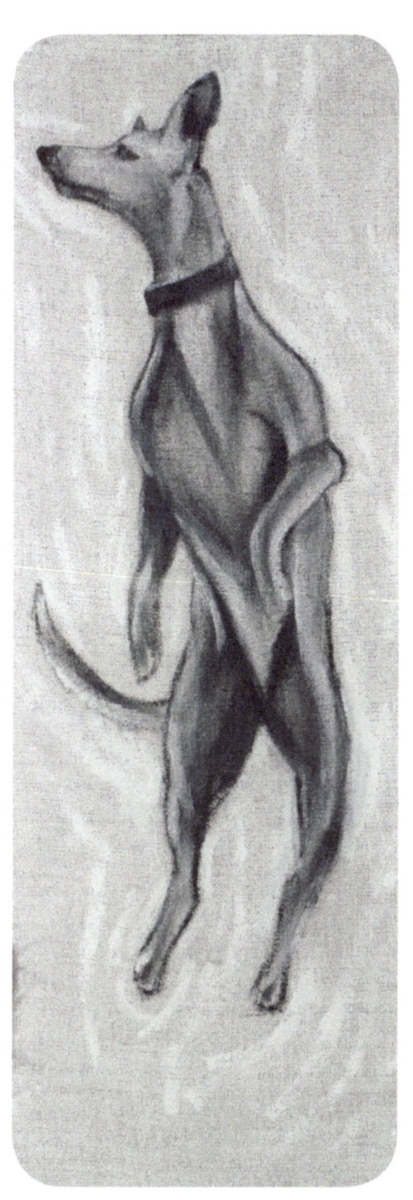

AMANDA HUGHES

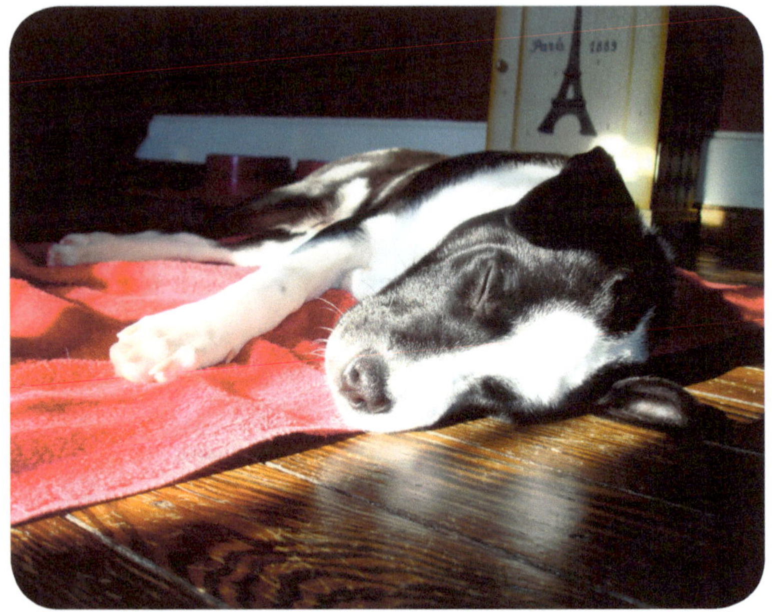

VICTORIA PATCHEN

In Washington, it's dog eat dog. In academia, it's exactly the opposite.

ROBERT REICH, (B. 1946)

The more I see of the representatives of the people, the more I admire my dogs.

ALPHONSE DE LAMARTINE, (1790-1869)

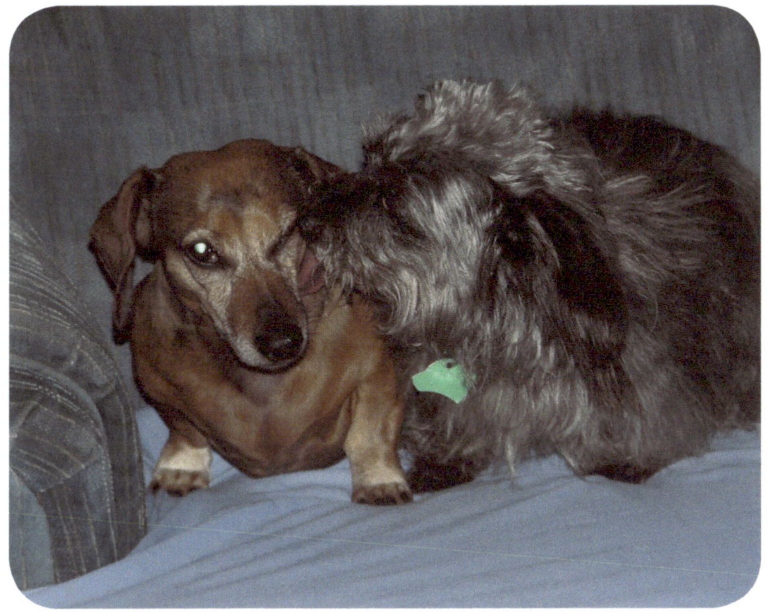

KARI HENNING

The dog is like a liberal. He wants to please everybody.

WILLIAM KUNSTLER, (1919-1995)

Dogmatism is puppyism come to its full growth.

DOUGLAS JERROLD, (1803-1857)

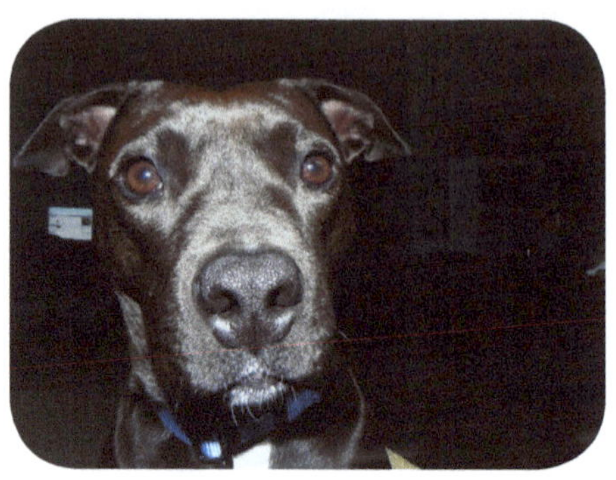

Jessica Galvin

Politics are not my concern… They impressed me as a dog's life without a dog's decencies.

Rudyard Kipling, (1865-1936)

America is a large friendly dog in a small room. Every time it wags its tail it knocks over a chair.

Arnold Toynbee, (1889-1975)

To his dog, every man is Napoleon; hence the constant popularity of dogs.

Aldous Huxley, (1884-1963)

The French are masters of "the dog ate my homework" school of diplomatic relations.

P.J. O'Rourke, (b. 1947)

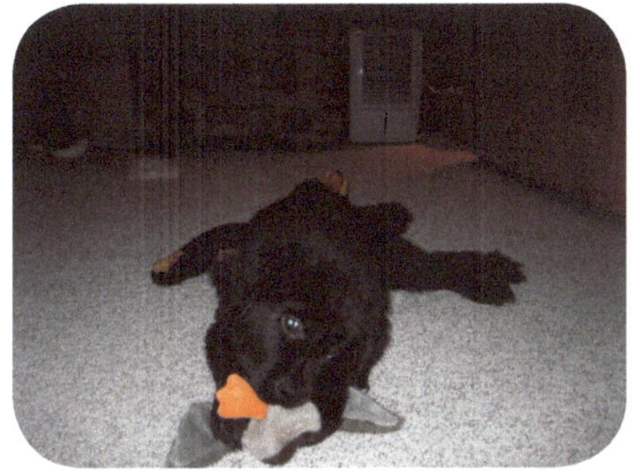

Kerri Bisner

What counts is not necessarily the size of the dog in the fight—it's the size of the fight in the dog.

Dwight D. Eisenhower, (1880-1959)

God did not make a hound-dog to scent out evil.

John Timothy Stone, (18??-19??)

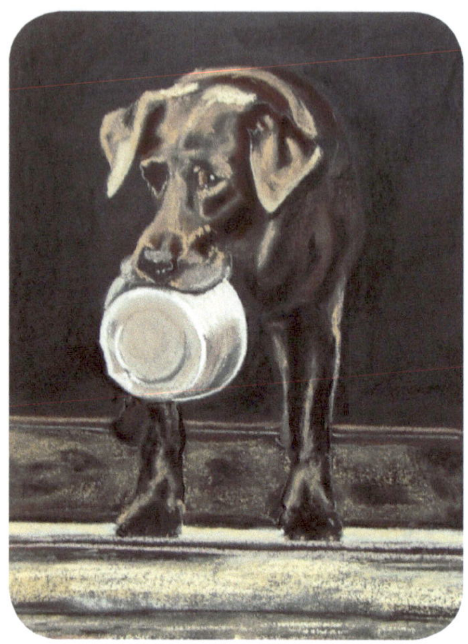

Celia Atkins

A dog starved at his master's gate Predicts the ruin of the state.

William Blake, (1757-1827)

Spending one's capital is feeding a dog on his own tail.

Mark Twain, (1935-1910)

Gratitude is a sickness suffered by dogs.

Joseph Stalin, (1878-1953)

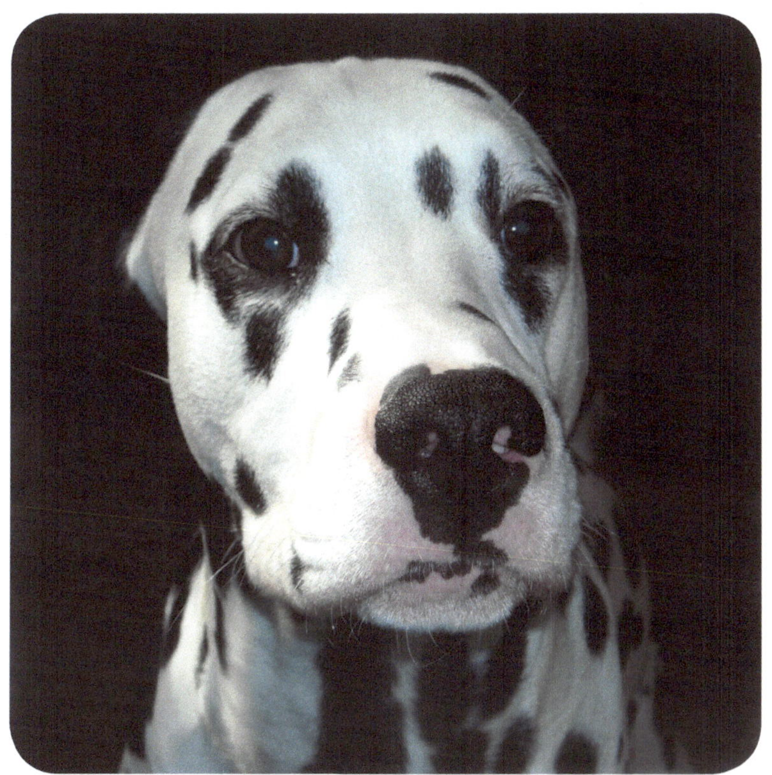

ELENA ANFALOVA

Every man is wise when attached by a mad dog; fewer when pursued by a mad woman; only the wisest survive when attacked by a mad notion.

ROBERTSON DAVIES, (1913-1995)

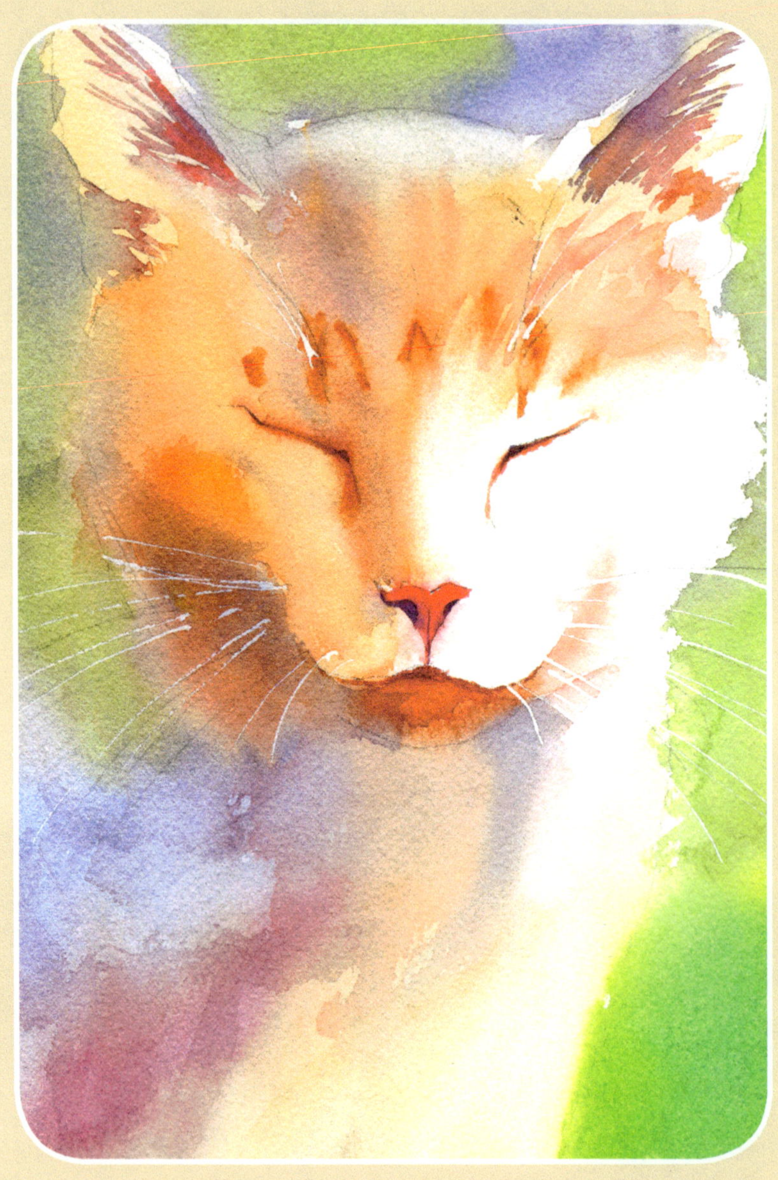

Rachel Parker

Chapter 3

Dogs vs Cats

Again I must remind you that A Dog's a Dog—A CAT'S A CAT.

T.S. Eliot, (1888-1965)

I like pigs. Dogs look up to us. Cats look down on us. Pigs treat us as equals.

Sir Winston Churchill, (1874-1965)

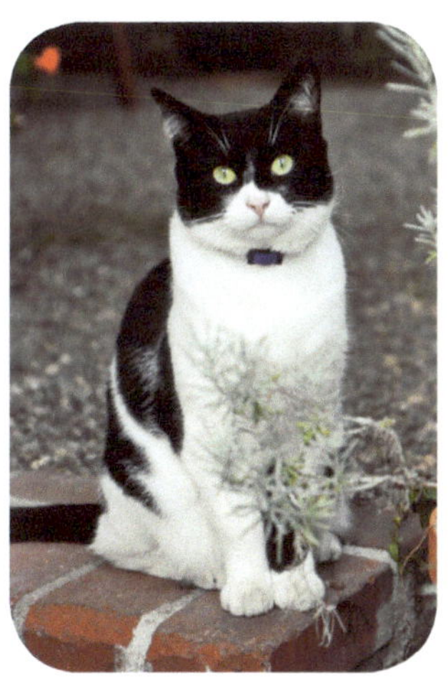

Abby Gregory

Let Hercules himself do what he may,
The cat will mew and dog will have his day.

William Shakespeare, (1564-1616)

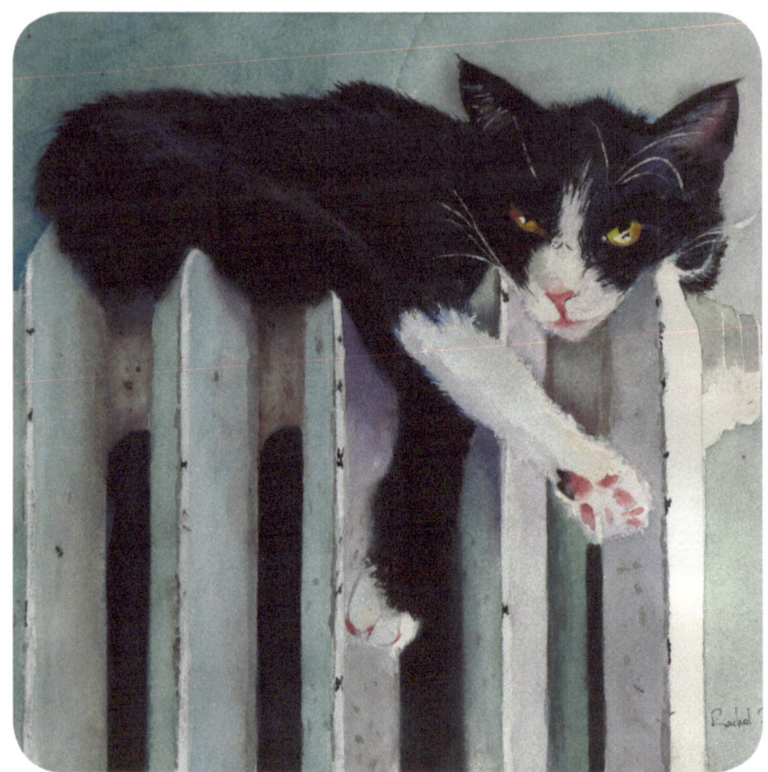

Rachel Parker

The real objection to the great majority of cats is their insufferable air of superiority.

P.G. Wodehouse, (1881-1975)

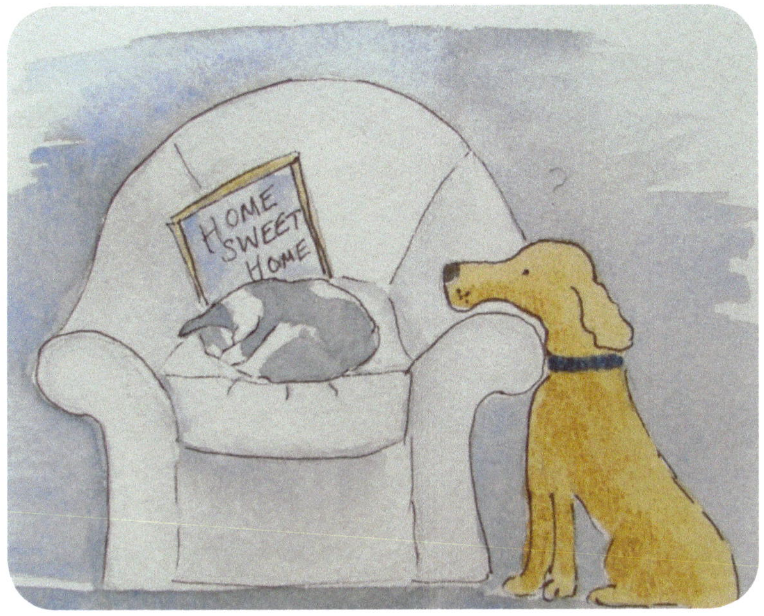

Celia Atkins

I have studied many philosophers and several cats. The wisdom of cats is vastly superior.

Hippolyte Taine, (1818-1893)

If animals could speak, the dog would be a blundering, outspoken, honest fellow—but the cat would have the rare grace of never saying a word too much.

Philip G. Hamerton, (1834-1894)

A cat has absolute emotional honesty: human beings, for one reason or another, may hide their feelings, but a cat does not.

Ernest Hemingway, (1899-1963)

If a cat spoke, it would say things like "Hey, I don't see the problem here".

Roy Blount, Jr., (b. 1941)

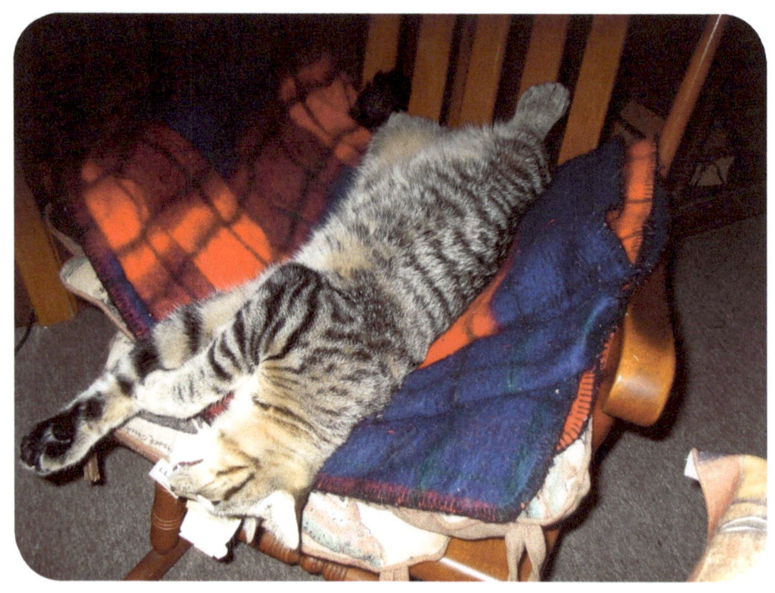

Kathy Carmichael

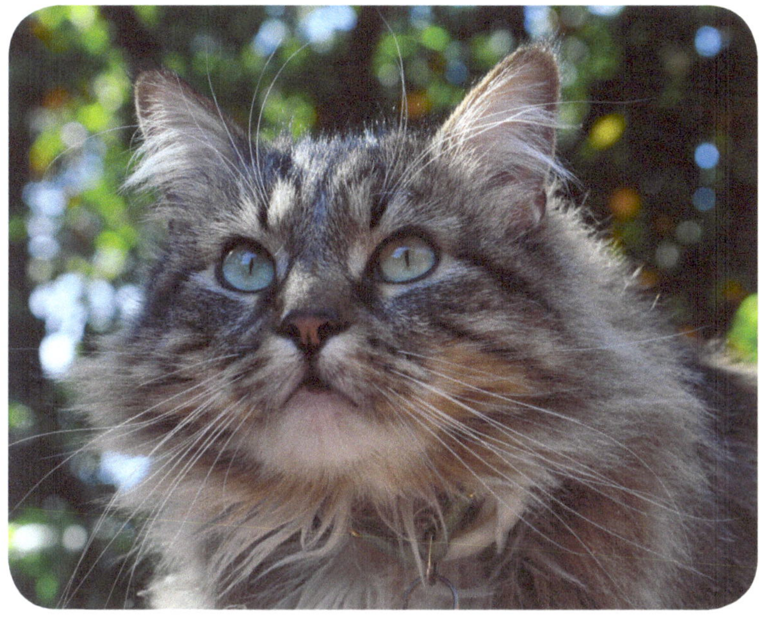

Gabrielle Utz

He who laugheth too much hath the nature of a fool; he that laugheth not at all hath the nature of an old cat.

Thomas Fuller I, (1907-1988)

Never try to outstubborn a cat.

Robert A. Heinlein, (1907-1968)

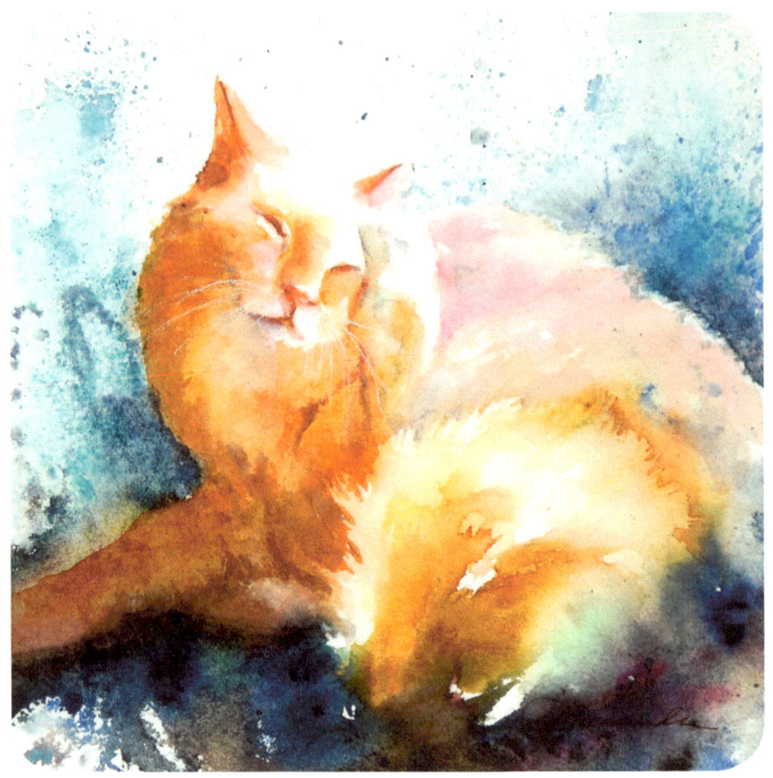

CANDACE FENANDER

Of all God's creatures there is only one that cannot be made the slave of the lash. That one is the cat. If man could be crossed with the cat, it would improve man, but it would deteriorate the cat.

MARK TWAIN, (1835-1910)

So it is, and such is life. The cat's away, and the mice they play.

CHARLES DICKENS, (1812-1870)

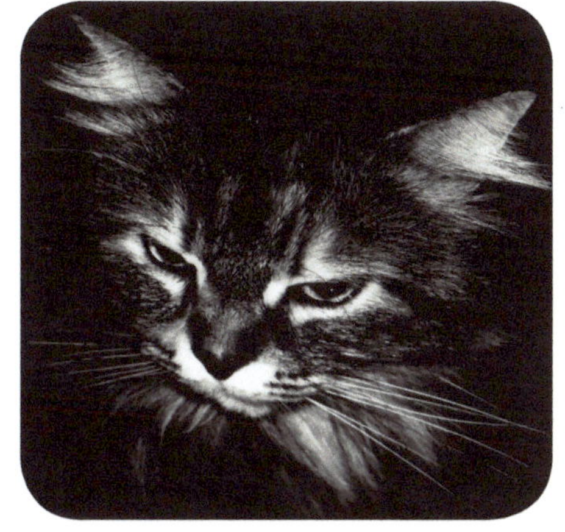

ELENA ANFALOVA

A man who carries a cat by the tail learns something he can learn in no other way.

MARK TWAIN, (1835-1910)

I think that it is to the cats' credit that neither Hitler nor Napoleon nor Alexander of Macedonia could belong [to cat-loving club]. They feared and hated cats. It is not recorded that a cat ever loved any of the lot, either.

ROGER A. CARAS, (1928-2001)

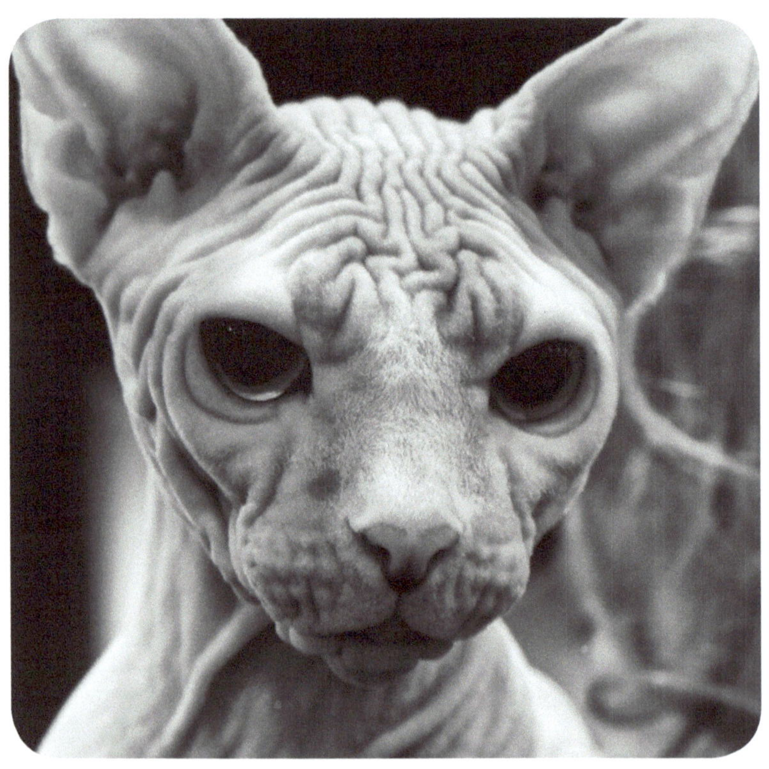

DONNA ROSSER

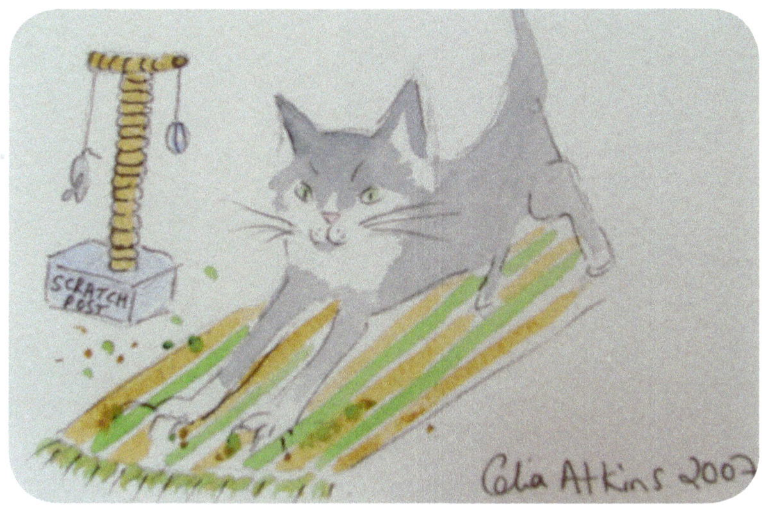

Celia Atkins

Everything that moves seems to interest and amuse a cat.

Francois Augustin-Paradis de Moncrif, (1687-1770)

The best mousetrap ever invented: a cat.

Evan Esar, (1899-1995)

Those who play with cats must expect to be scratched.

Miguel De Cervantes, (1547-1616)

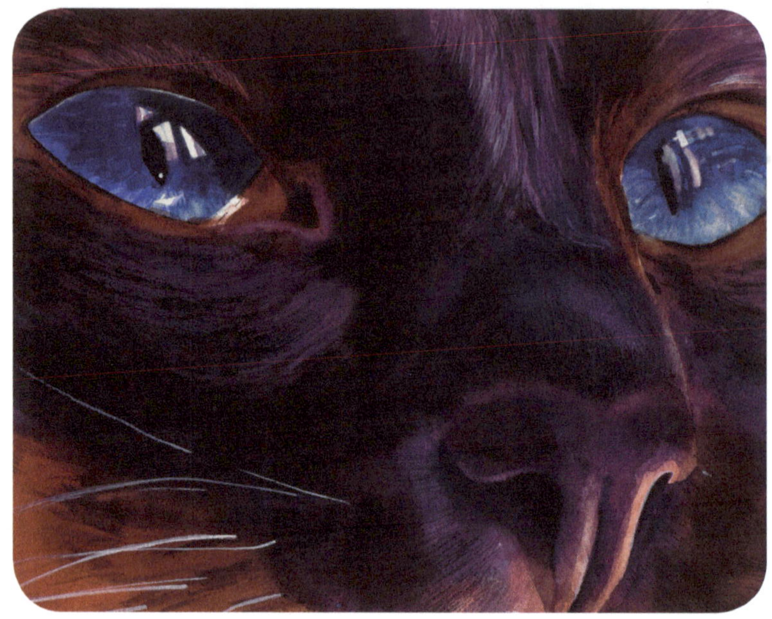

RACHEL PARKER

Only a Frenchman can understand the fine and subtle qualities of the cat.

THEOPHILE GAUTIER, (1811-1872)

Artist like cats; soldiers like dogs.

DESMOND MORRIS, (B. 1928)

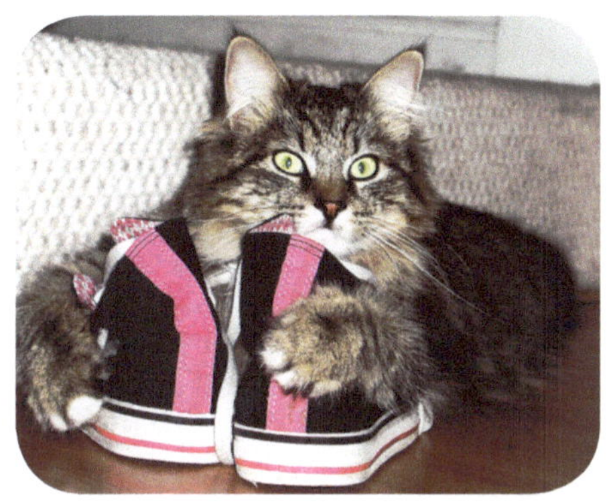

GABRIELLE UTZ

In order to keep a true perspective of one's importance, everyone should have a dog that will worship him and a cat that will ignore him.

DEREKE BRUCE, (?)

The vanity of man revolts from the serene indifference of the cat.

AGNES REPPLIER, (1855-1950)

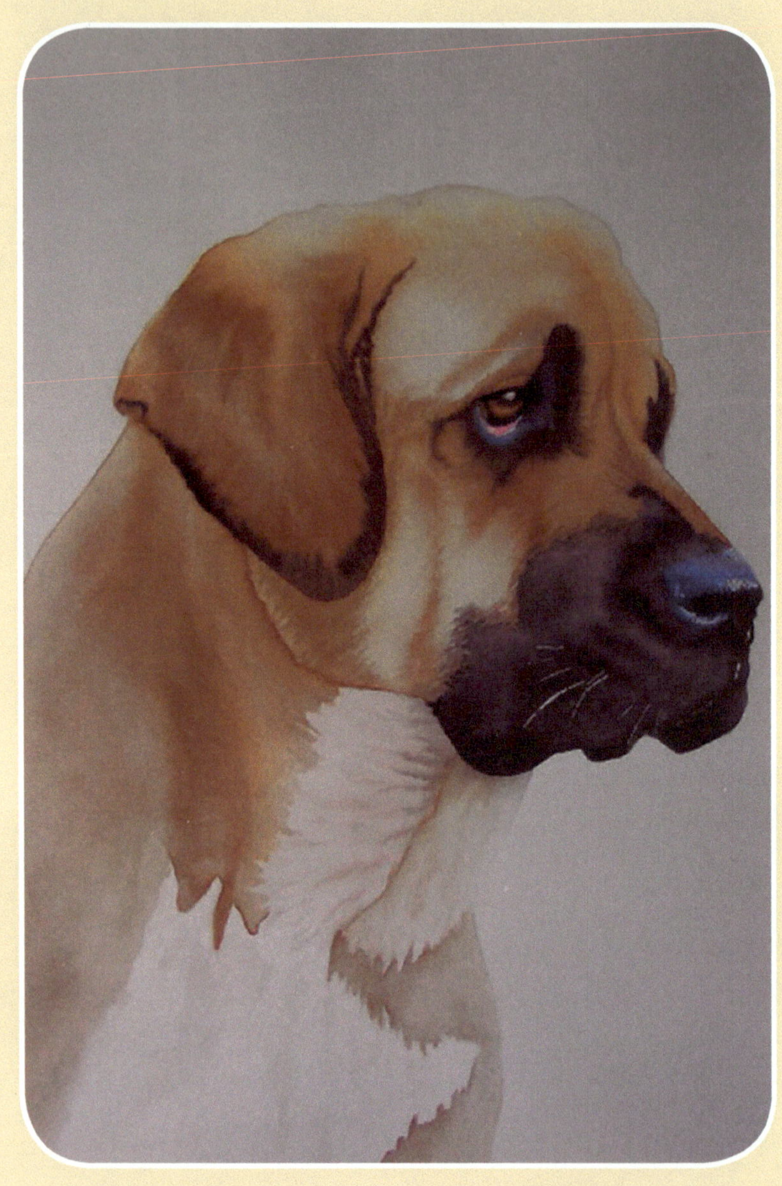

Kathryn Ragan

Chapter 4

Dogs & Religion

I care not for a man's religion whose dog and cat are not the better for it.

Abraham Lincoln, (1809-1865)

God give to me by your grace what you give to dogs by nature.

Mechtilda of Magdeberg, (1207-1282)

The dog is a gentleman; I hope to go to his heaven, not man's.

Mark Twain, (1835-1910)

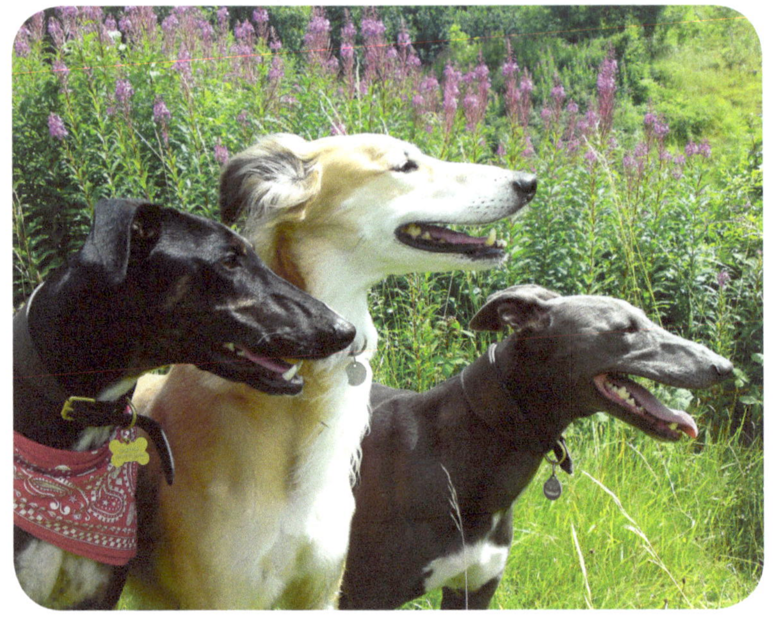

ABBY GREGORY

Our German forefathers had a very kind religion. They believed that, after death, they would meet again all the good dogs that had been their companions in life. I wish I could believe that too.

OTTO VON BISMARCK, (1815-1898)

If my dog is barred by the heavenly guard We'll both of us brave the heat!

W. DAYTON WEDGEFARTH, (?)

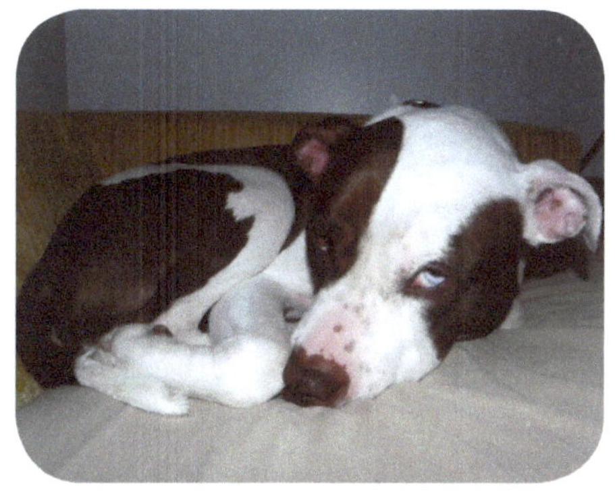

JESSICA GALVIN

When the dog was created, it licked the hand of God and God stroked its head, saying, *"What do you want, dog?"* It replied, *"My Lord, I want to stay with you, in heaven, on a mat in front of the gate..."*

MARIE NOEL, (1883-1967)

I have always felt it was human arrogance that assumes that only people have souls.

ANNE RAVER, (B.19??)

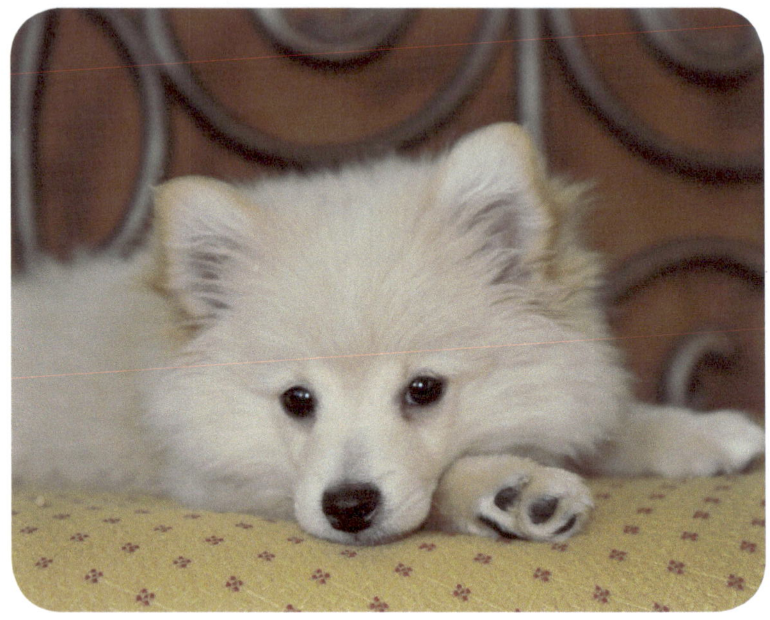

Gabrielle Utz

Be comforted, little dog, thou too in the Resurrection shall have a tail of gold.

Martin Luther, (1438-1546)

Heaven goes by favor. If it went by merit you would stay out and the dog would go in.

Mark Twain, (1835-1910)

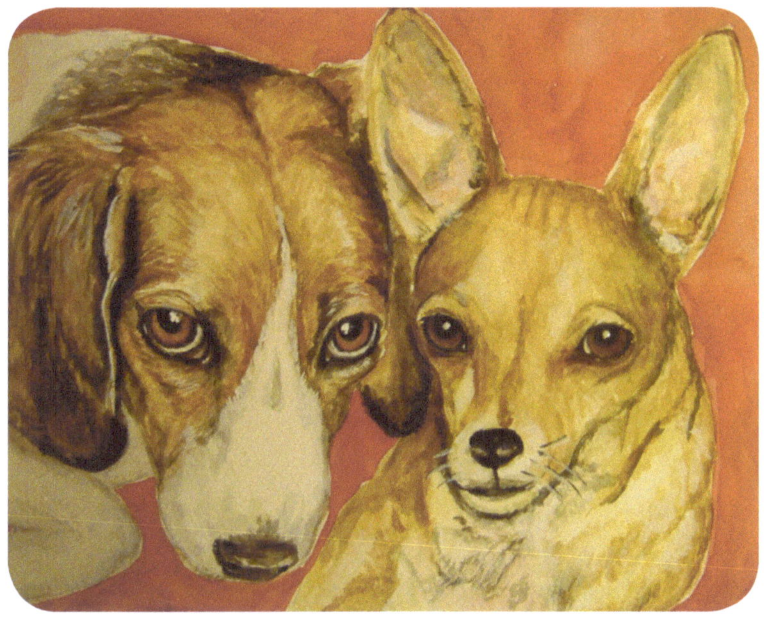

PAMELA UTTON

I don't believe in the concept of hell, but if I did I would think of it as filled with people who were cruel to animals.

GARY LARSON, (B. 1950)

If I have any beliefs about immortality, it is that certain dogs I have known will go to heaven, and very, very few persons.

JAMES THURBER, (1894-1961)

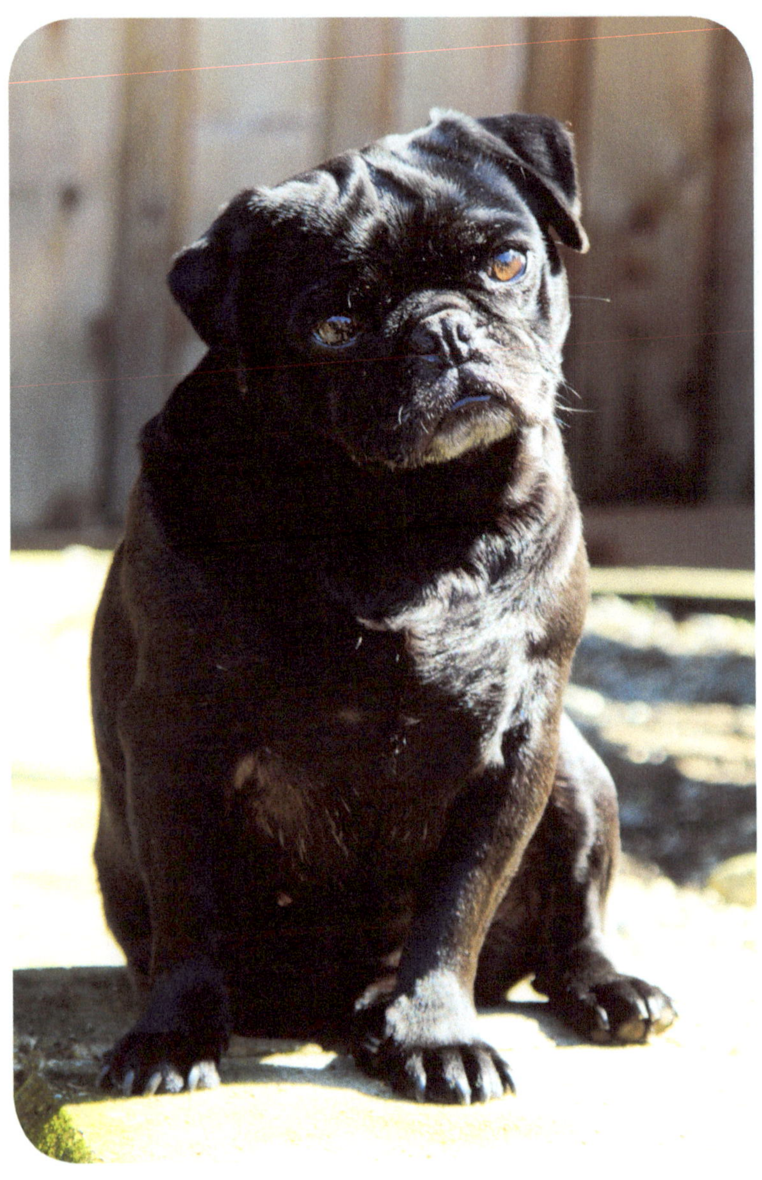

Kary Kidder

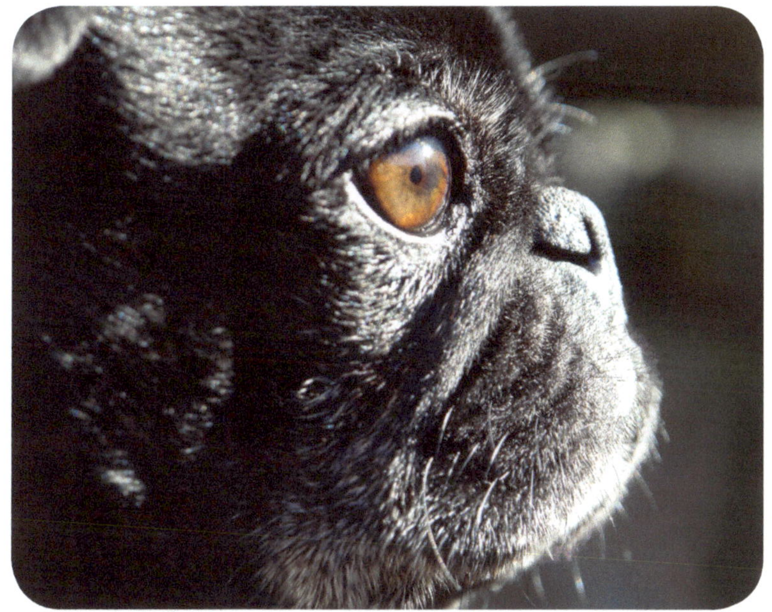

Kary Kidder

The pug is living proof that God has a sense of humor.

Margo Kaufman, (1953-2000)

My father was a St. Bernard, my mother was a Collie, but I am a Presbyterian. That is what my mother told me; I do not know these nice distinctions myself.

Mark Twain, (1835-1910)

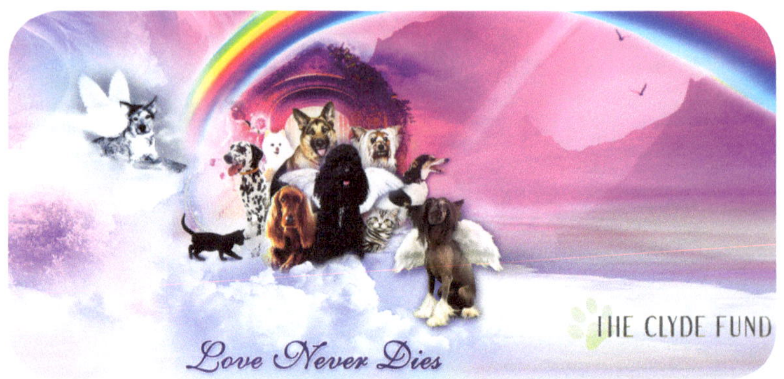

CLYDE VAN SAVAGE

You think dogs will not be in heaven? I tell you, they will be there before any of us.

ROBERT LOUIS STEVENSON, (1850-1894)

Reverence: the spiritual attitude of a man to a god and a dog to a man.

AMBROSE BIERCE, (1842-1914)

Who loves me will love my dog also.

ST. BERNARD OF CLAIRVAUX, (1090-1153)

Ah, if I could only pray the way that dog looks at meat.

MARTIN LUTHER, (1438-1546)

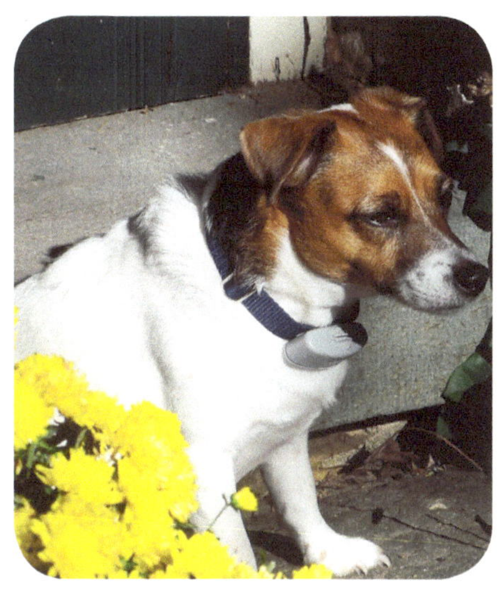

WILLIAM TRAVIS

Dogs do have many advantages over people, but one of them is extremely important: euthanasia is not forbidden by law in their cases; animals have the right to a merciful death.

MILAN KUNDERA, (B.1929)

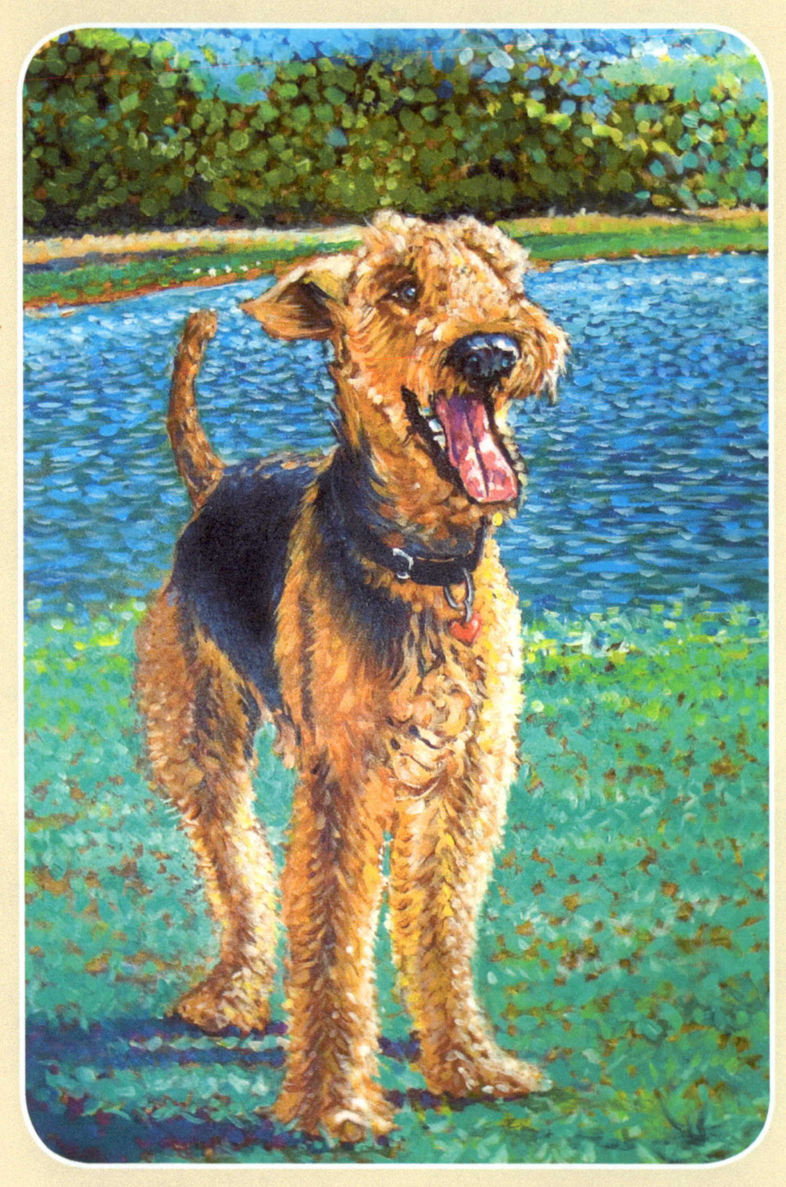

Kevin Rockwell

Chapter 5

Dog Humor

Scratch a dog and you'll find a permanent job.

Franklin P. Jones, (1887-1929)

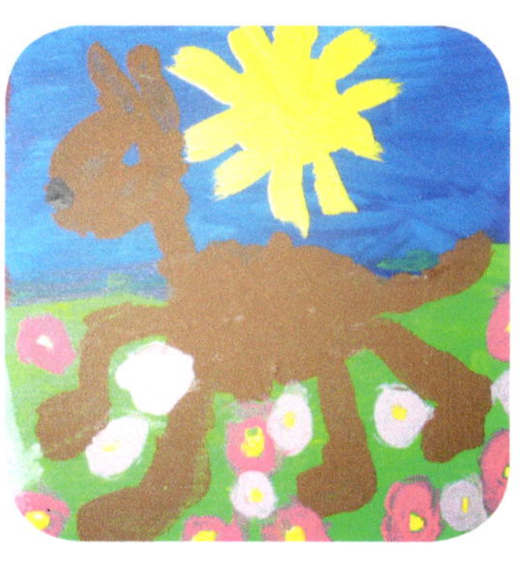

Dylan Cunningham

Outside of a dog, a book is man's best friend. Inside of a dog, it's too dark to read.

Groucho Marx, (1890-1977)

I am an old dog, and *tus, tus,* will not do for me.

Miguel de Cervantes, (1547-1616)

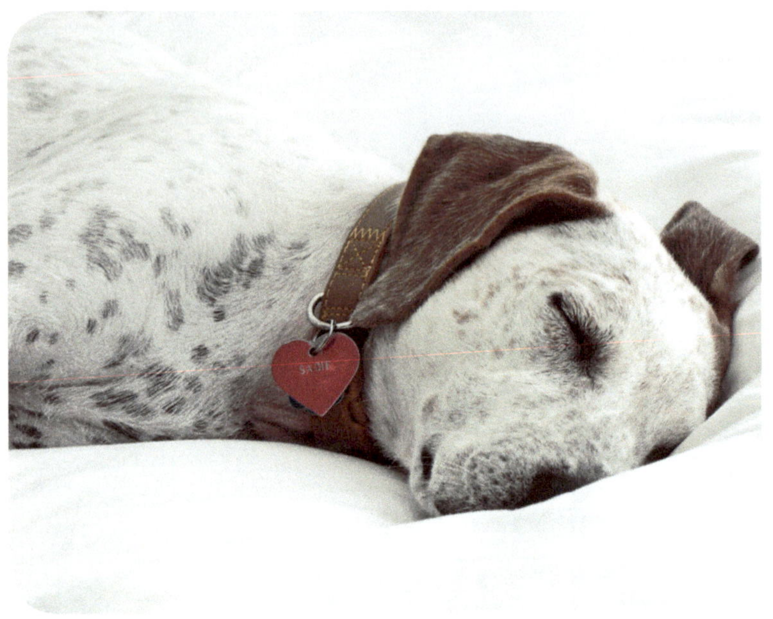

Donna Rosser

Just give me a comfortable couch, a dog, a good book and a woman. Then if you can get the dog to go somewhere and read the book, I might have a little fun.

Groucho Marx, (1890-1977)

I looked up my family tree and found three dogs using it.

Rodney Dangerfield, (1921-2004)

CHAPTER 5

DOG HUMOR

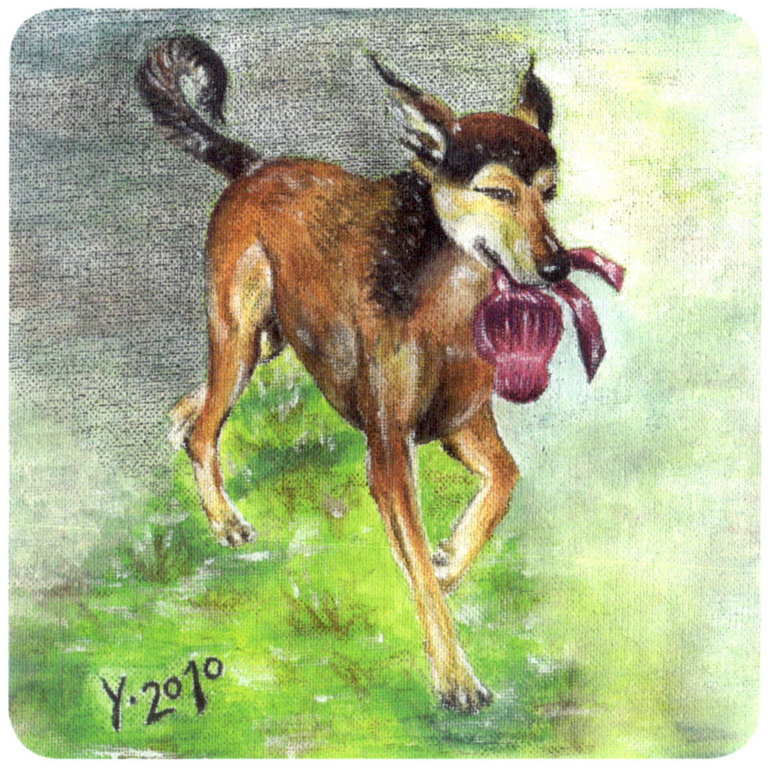

Yvonne Lautenschlager

Diamonds are a girl's best friend. Dogs are a man's best friend. Now you know which sex is smarter.

Nancy Gray, (b.19??)

If you are a dog and your owner suggests that you wear a sweater… suggest that he wear a tail.

FRAN LEBOWITZ, (B. 1951)

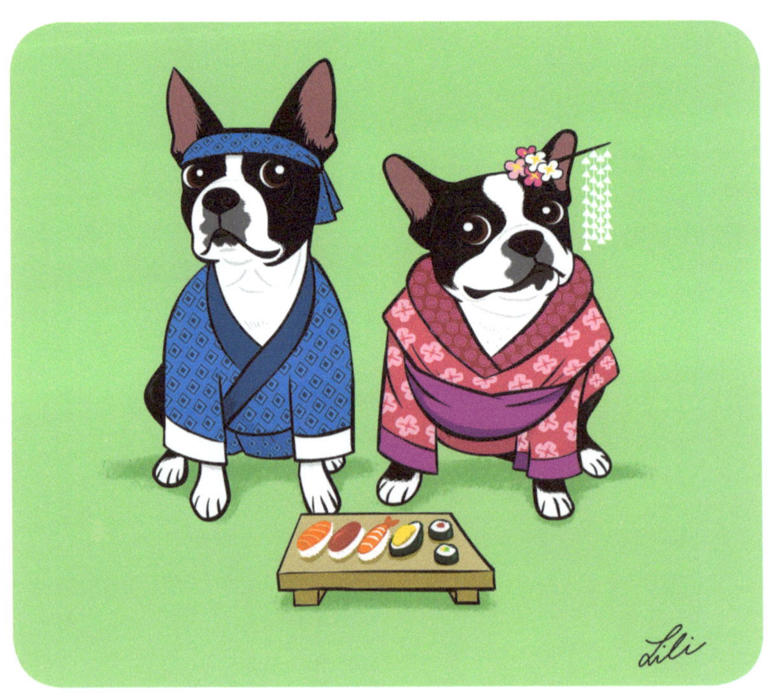

LILI CHIN

On the Internet, nobody knows you're a dog.

Peter Steiner, 1917-2007)

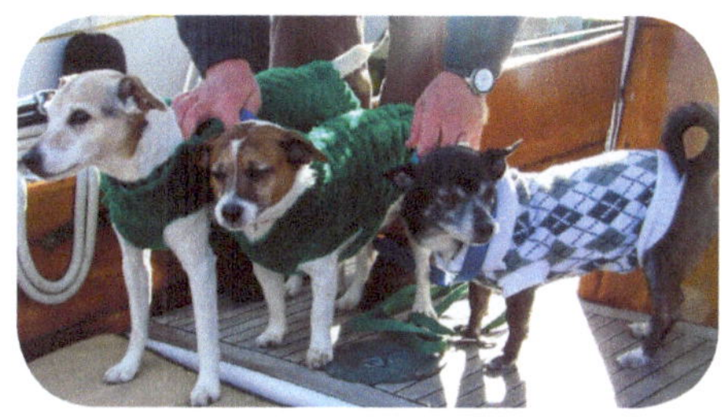

William Travis

The dog is a yes-animal, very popular with people who can't afford to keep a yes-man.

Robertson Davies, (1913-1995)

The cocktail party—as the name itself indicates—was originally invented by dogs. They are simply bottom-sniffings raised to the rank of formal ceremonies.

Lawrence Durrell, (1912-1990)

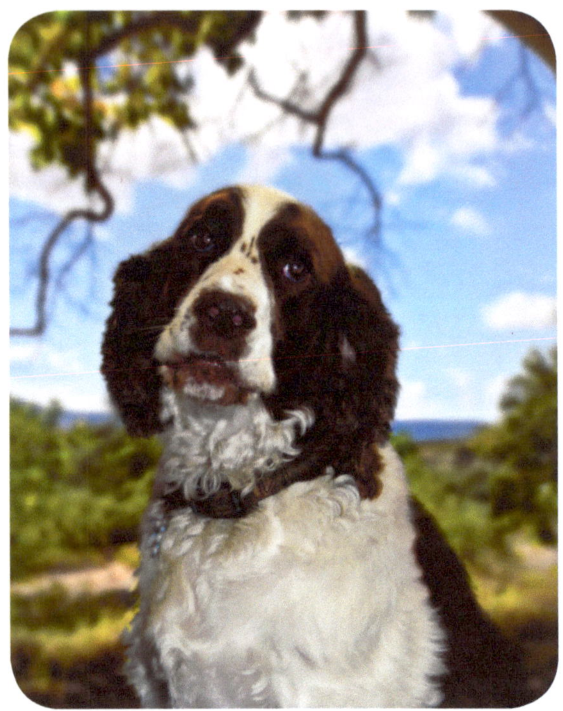

JEAN HILDEBRANT

Don't accept your dog's admiration as conclusive evidence that you are wonderful.

ANN LANDERS (1918-2002)

FOOVIEW (foo'view) n. The ability of a dog to inflict guilt from any angle in the room while he watches his master eat.

RICH HALL, (B. 1954)

CHAPTER 5

DOG HUMOR

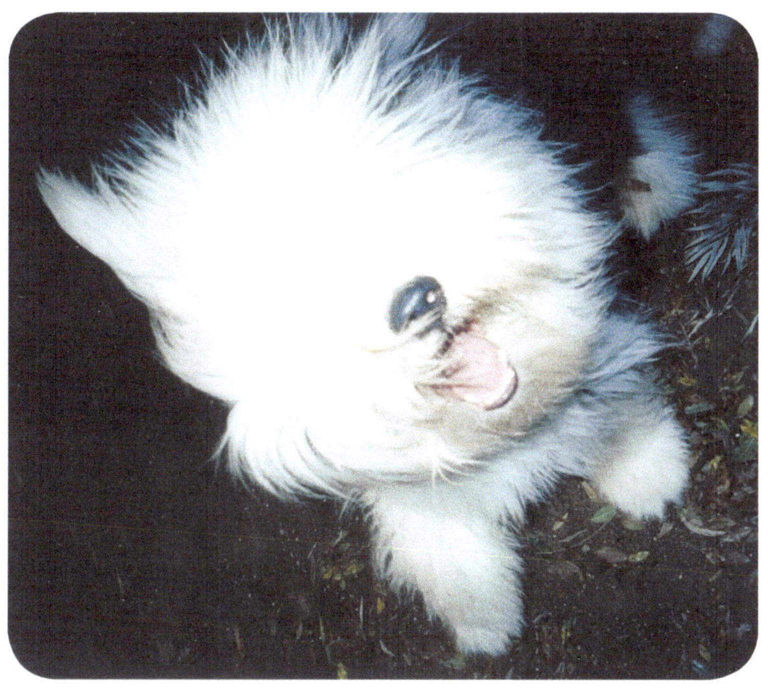

Patricia Denys

The advantages of whiskey over dogs are legion. Whiskey does not need to be periodically wormed, it does not need to be fed, it never requires a special kennel, it has no toenails to be clipped or coat to be stripped. Whiskey sits quietly in its special nook until you want it. True, whiskey has a nasty habit of running out, but then so does a dog.

W. C. Fields, (1880-1946)

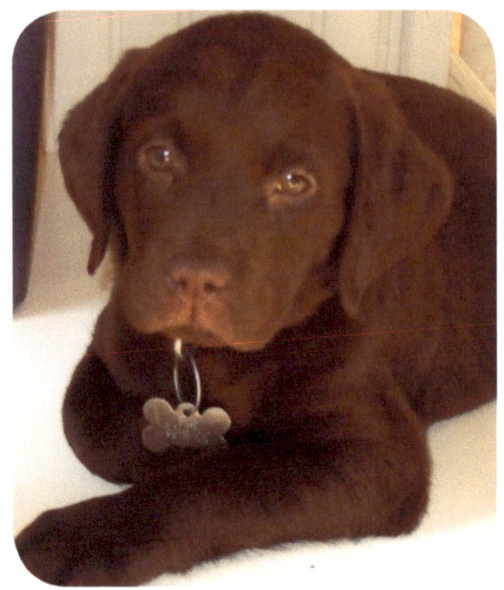

Robby Glass

The other day a dog peed on me. A bad sign.

H. L. Mencken, (1880-1956)

Yesterday I was a dog. Today I'm a dog. Tomorrow I'll probably still be a dog. Sigh! There's so little hope for advancement.

Charles M. Schulz, (1922-2000), (Snoopy)

It is fatal to let any dog know that he is funny, for he immediately loses his head and starts hamming it up.

P. G. Wodehouse, (1881-1975)

CHAPTER 5

DOG HUMOR

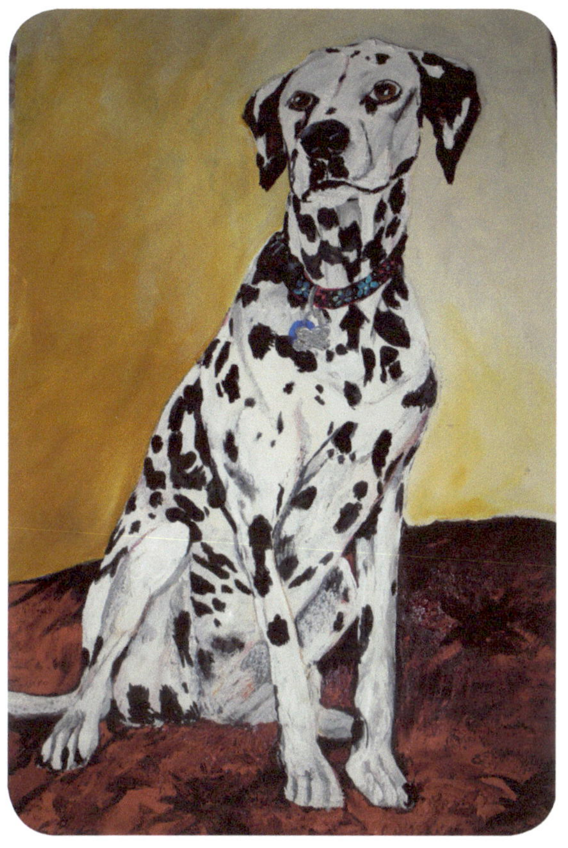

Kylie Farrelly

My husband and I are either going to buy a dog or have a child. We can't decide whether to ruin our carpets or ruin our lives.

Rita Rudner, (b.1955)

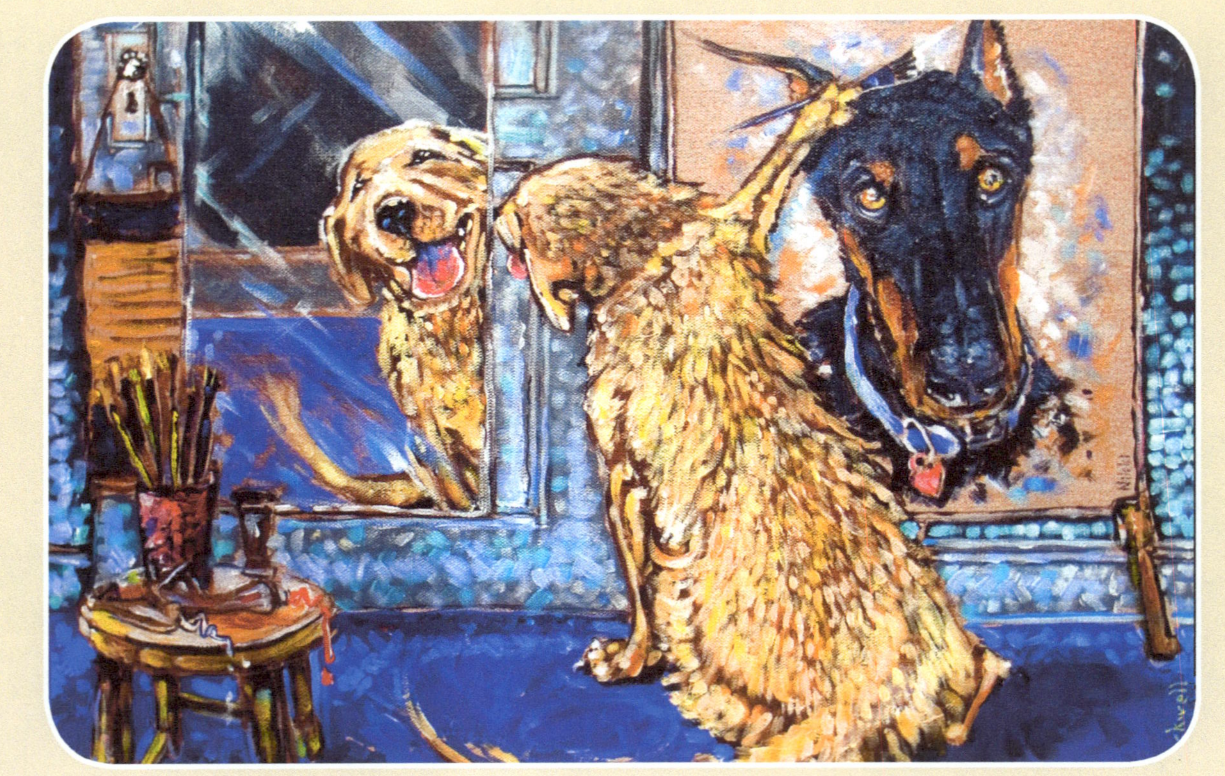

Nikkis Self Portrait Kevin Rockwell

Chapter 6

Of Dogs & Men

If you can resist treating a rich friend better than a poor friend,
If you can face the world without lies and deceit,
If you can say honestly that deep in your heart you have no prejudice against creed, color, religion or politics,
Then, my friend, you are almost as good as your dog.

Author unknown

Histories are more full of examples of the fidelity of dog than of friends.

Alexander Pope, (1688-1744)

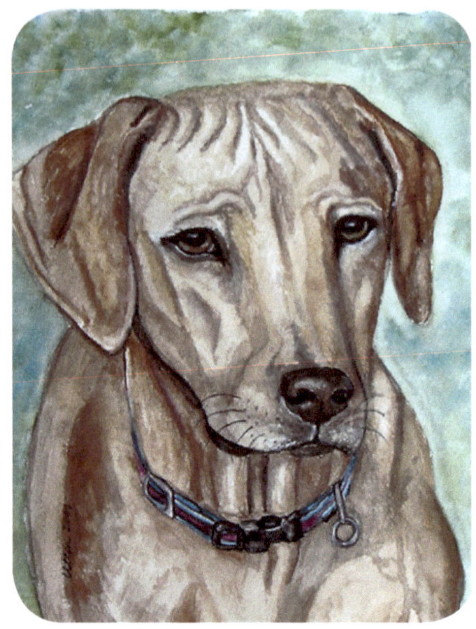

Pamela Utton

If you pick up a starving dog and make him prosperous, he will not bite you. This is the primary difference between a dog and a man.

Mark Twain, (1835-1910)

Dogs love their friends and bite their enemies, quite unlike people who are incapable of pure love and always have to mix love and hate in their object relations.

Sigmund Freud, (1856-1939)

The more I see of men, the more I admire dogs.

JEANNE-MARIE ROLAND, (1754-1793)

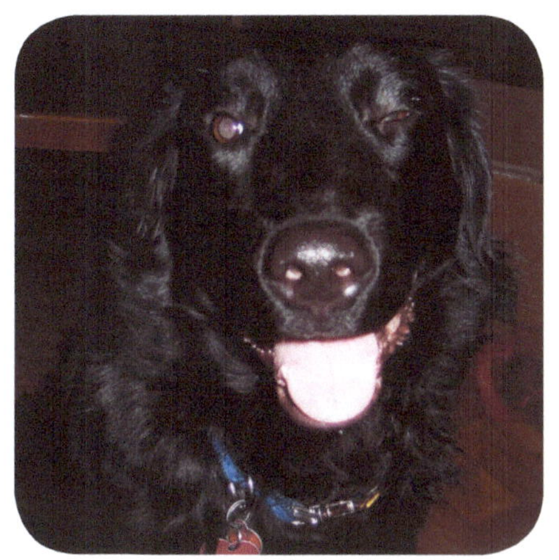

MARIA DE LEON

He cannot be a gentleman which loveth not a dog.

JOHN NORTHBROOKE, (1567-1589)

To be a high-mannered and high-minded gentleman, careless, affable, and gay, is the inborn pretension of the dog.

ROBERT LOUIS STEVENSON, (1850-1894)

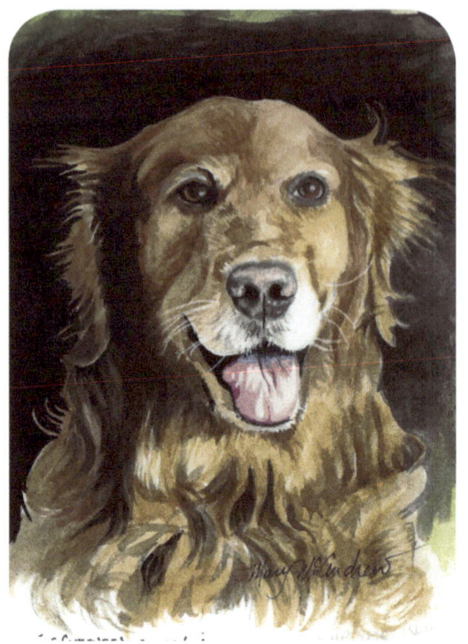

MARY MCANDREWS

I had rather hear my dog bark at a crow than a man swear he loves me.

WILLIAM SHAKESPEARE, (1564-1616)

Some of my best leading men have been dogs and horses.

ELIZABETH TAYLOR, (B. 1932)

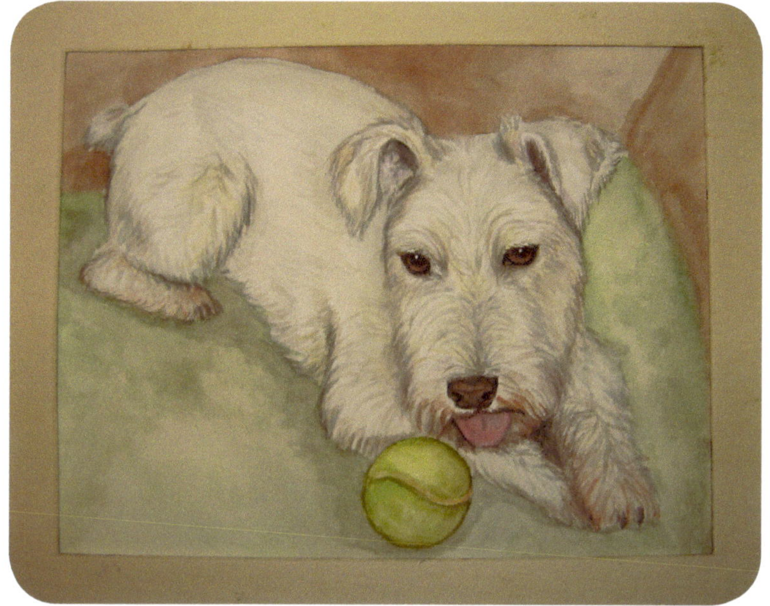

PAMELA UTTON

Dogs never bite me. Just humans.

MARILYN MONROE, (1926-1962)

I wish all men were like dogs.

HALLE BERRY, (B. 1966)

Men cheat for the same reason that dogs lick their balls... because they can.

KIM CATTRALL, (B. 1956)

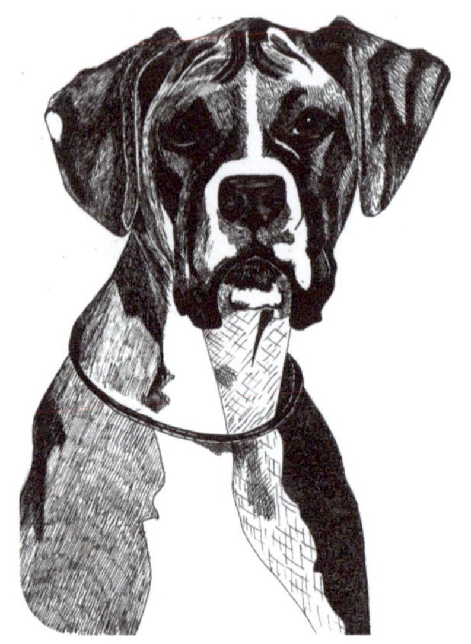

Evelyn Grant

As a wolf is like a dog, so is a flatterer like a friend.

Thomas Fuller, (1608-1661)

There are three faithful friends—an old wife, an old dog, and ready money.

Benjamin Franklin, (1706-1790)

When a man's dog turns against him it is time for his wife to pack her trunk and go home to mamma.

Mark Twain, (1835-1910)

CHAPTER 6

OF DOGS & MEN

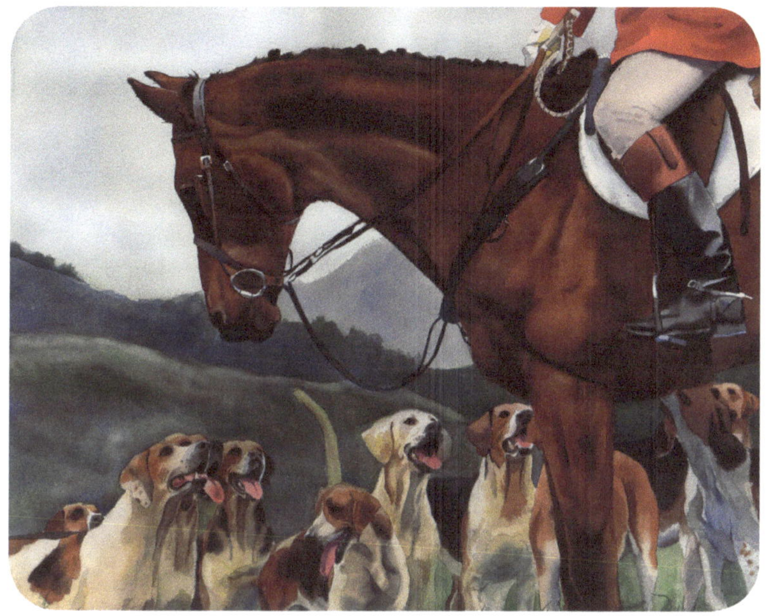

Rachel Parker

Men are generally more careful of the breed of their horses and dogs than of their children.

William Penn, (1644-1718)

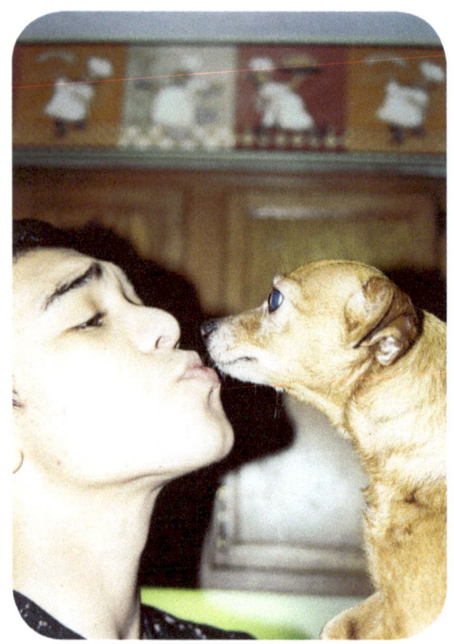

Every puppy should have a boy.

Erma Bombeck, (1927-1996)

Jay Jude

I know that I have had friends who would never have vexed or betrayed me, if they had walked on all fours.

Horace Walpole, (1717-1797)

When a dog runs at you, whistle for him.

Henry David Thoreau, (1817-1862)

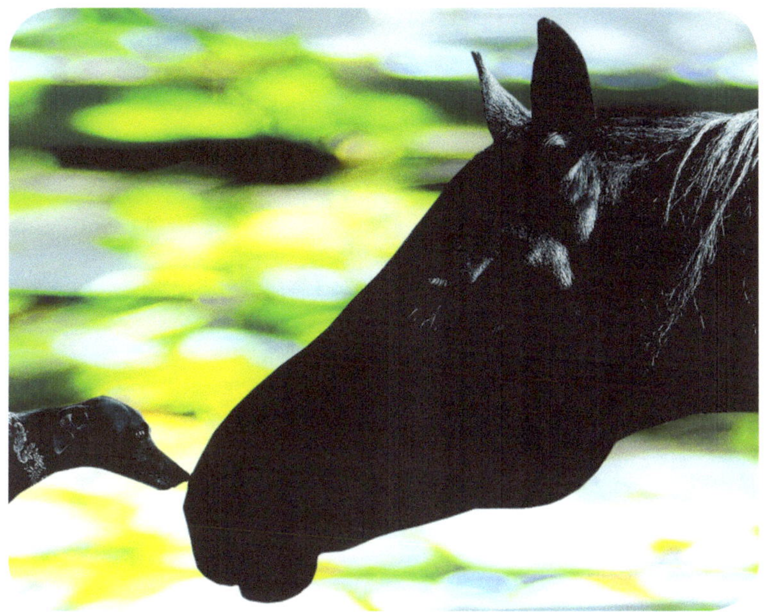

Anja Hammefahr

Nothing like blood, sir, in hosses, dawgs, and men.

William Makepeace Thackeray,
(1811-1863)

Brothers and Sisters, I bid you beware
Of giving your heart to a dog to tear.

Rudyard Kipling, (1865-1936)

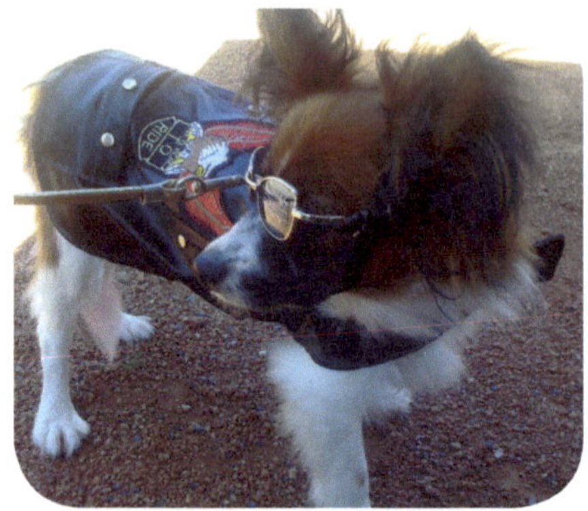

Penny Lindh

Dog lovers are a good breed themselves.

Gladys Taber, (1899-1980)

Women and cats do as they damned well please, and men and dog had best learn to live with it.

Alan Holbrook, (?)

There are no wild animals till man makes them so.

Mark Twain, (1835-1910)

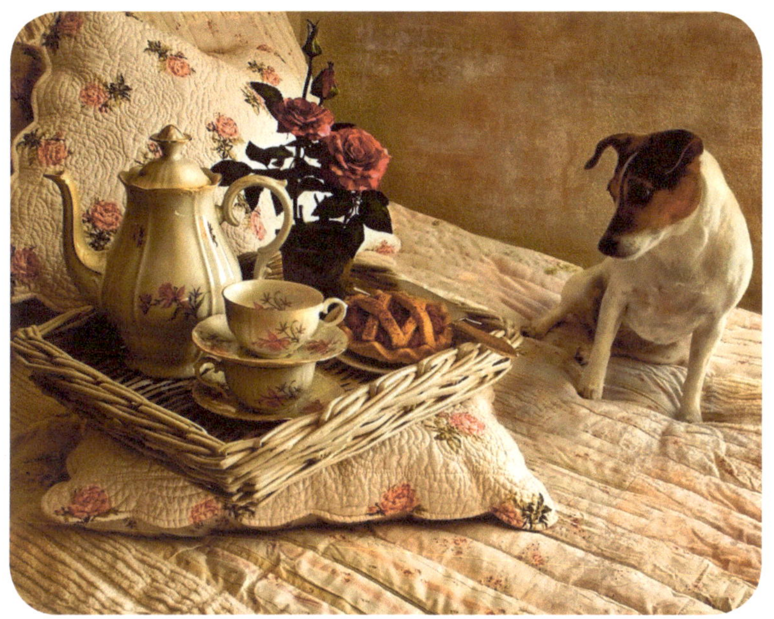

Jean Hildebrant

There are no one-night stands for a dog. Once you let your pet into your bed, it's hard to get him out.

Diana Delmar, (b.19??)

If a dog will not come to you after having looked you in the face, you should go home and examine your conscience.

Woodrow Wilson, (1856-1924)

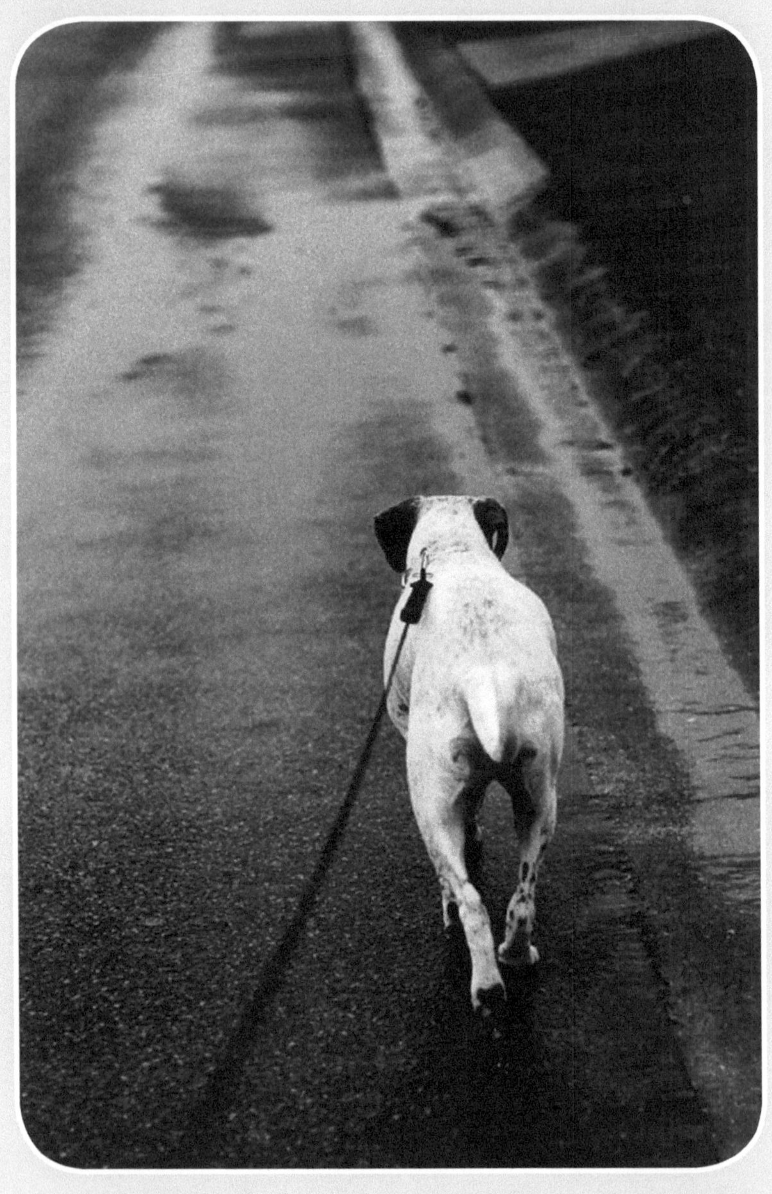

Donna Rosser

Chapter 7

Death of a Friend

In his grief over the loss of a dog, a little boy stands for the first time on tiptoe, peering into the rueful morrow of manhood. After this most inconsolable of sorrows there is nothing life can do to him that he will not be able to somehow bear.

James Thurber, (1894-1961)

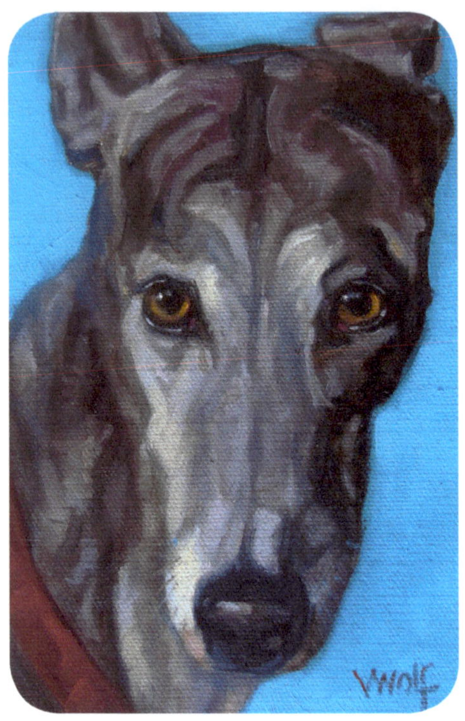

VALARIE WOLF

I guess you don't really own a dog, you rent them, and you have to be thankful that you had a long lease.

JOE GARAGIOLA, (B. 1926)

The one best place to bury a good dog is in the heart of his master.

BEN HUR LAMPMAN, (1886-1954)

Dogs' lives are too short. Their only fault, really.

AGNES SLIGH TURNBULL, (1888-1982)

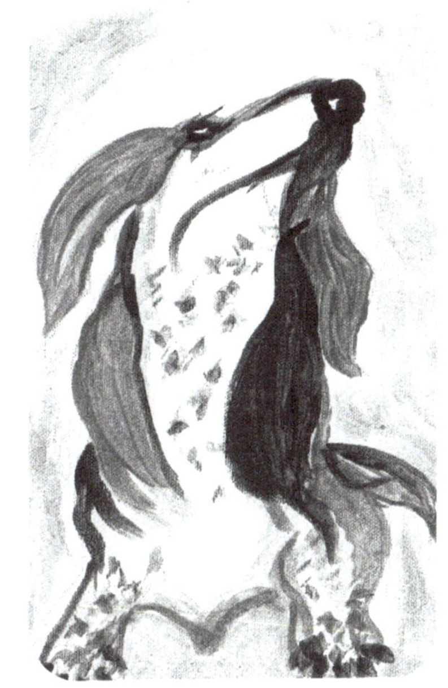

SUE CAROLINE OGDEN

Old men miss many dogs.

STEVE ALLEN, (1921-2000)

The best way to get over a dog's death is to get another soon.

RONALD REAGAN, (1911-2004)

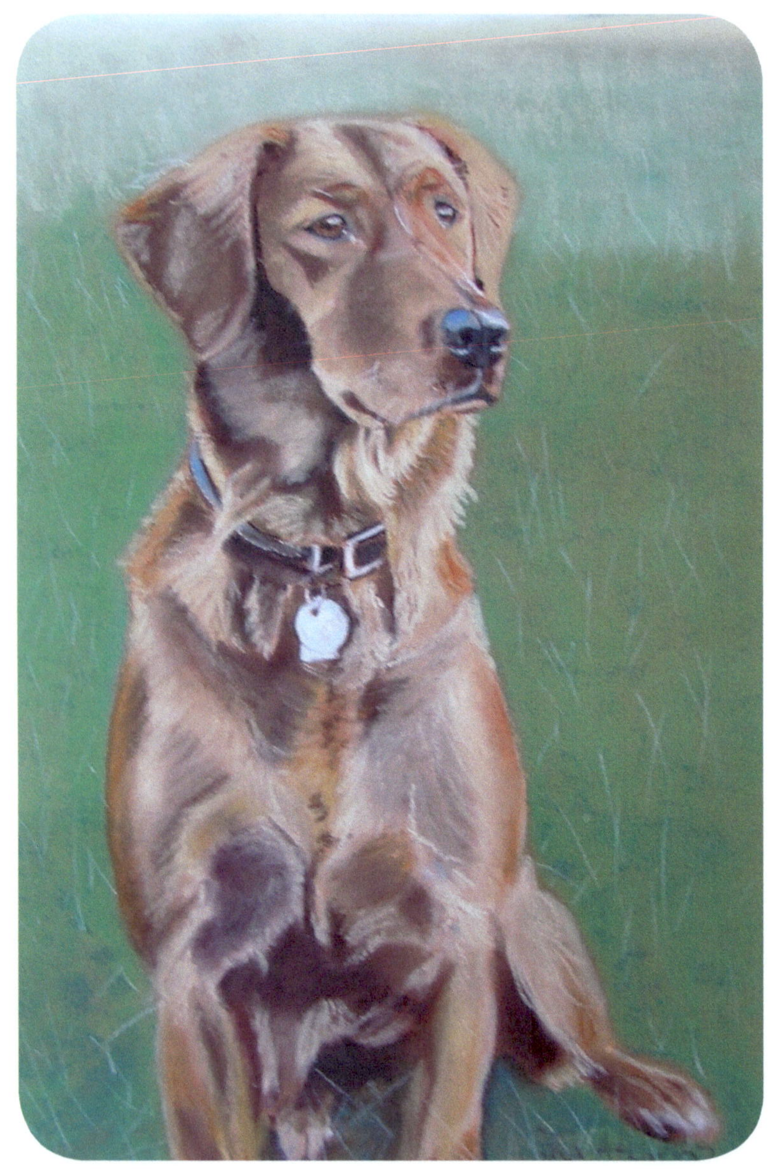

Celia Atkins

CHAPTER 7

DEATH OF A FRIEND

Old Blue died and he died so hard
I dug the ground in my back yard
Lowered him down with a silver chain
Every link I did call his name.
Blue, oh Blue
You good dog, you.

When I go to heaven
I know what I'll do.
I'll take my horn
And I'll blow for Blue.
Blue, oh Blue
I'm a'coming there, too.

Anonymous, "Old Blue," folk song

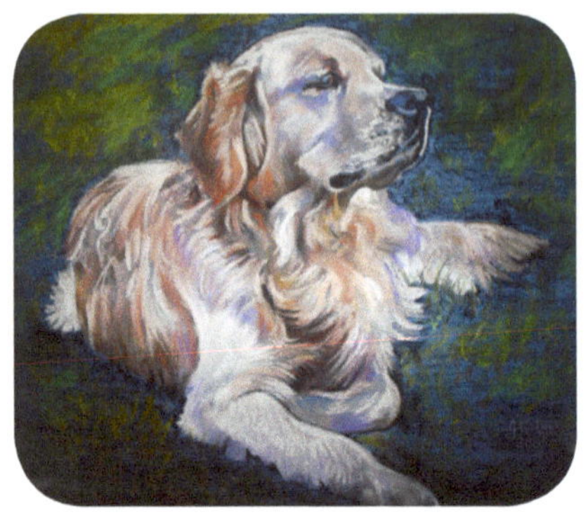

Gill Low

The old dog barks backward without getting up. I can remember when he was a pup.

Robert Frost, (1874-1963)

I have sometimes thought of the final cause of dogs having such short lives and I am quite satisfied it is in compassion to the human race; for if we suffer so much in losing a dog after an acquaintance of ten or twelve years, what would it be if they were to live double that time?

Sir Walter Scott, (1771-1823)

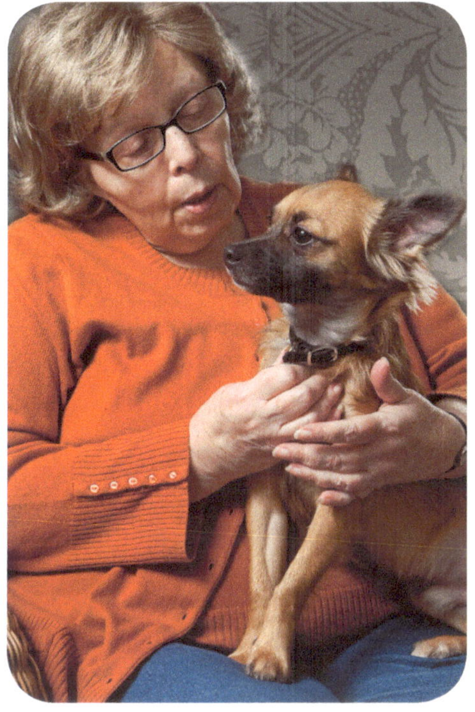

SUSAN GERTZ

It is a terrible thing for an old woman to outlive her dogs.

TENNESSEE WILLIAMS, (1911-1983)

Not the least hard thing to bear when they go from us, these quiet friends, is that they carry away with them so many years of our own lives.

JOHN GALSWORTHY, (1867-1933)

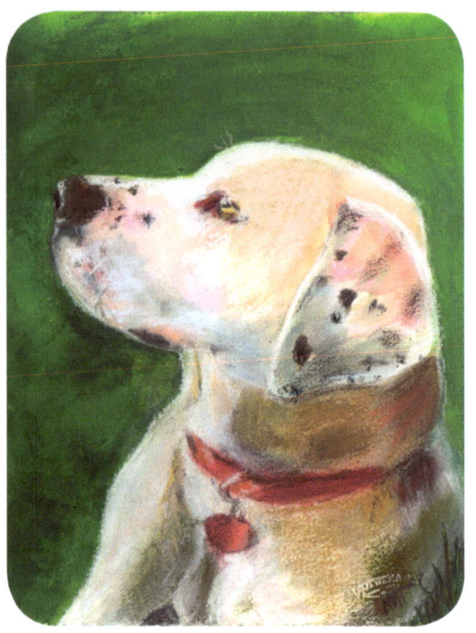

KAREN TRAVIS

Ten years ago she split the air
To seize what she could spy;
Tonight she bumps against a chair,
Betrayed by milky eye.
She seems to pant, Time up, time up!
My little dog must die,
And lie in dust with hector's pup;
So, presently, must I.

OGDEN NASH, (1902-1971)

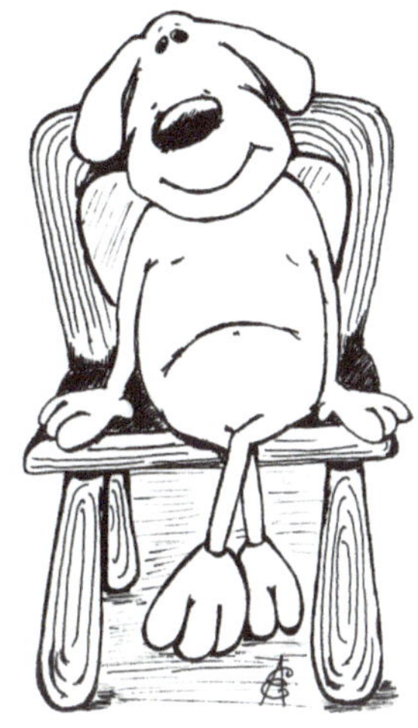

ELENA ANFALOVA

Be with me, Beauty, for
the fire is dying;
My dog and I are old,
too old for roving.

JOHN MASEFIELD, (1878-1967)

No louder shrieks to
pitying heaven are cast,
when husbands or lap-dogs
breathe their last.

ALEXANDER POPE, (1688-1744)

Animals have these advantages over man:
They have no theologians to instruct them,
their funerals cost them nothing, and no one
starts lawsuits over their wills.

VOLTAIRE, (1694-1778)

Epitaths

At thieves, I bark'd, at lovers wagg'd my tail,
And thus I pleased both Lord and Lady Frail.

JOHN WILKES, (1727-1797)

Here lies DASH, the Favorite Spaniel of
Queen Victoria
By whose command this Memorial was Erected.
He died on the 20 December, 1840 in his 9th year.
His attachment was without selfishness,
His playfulness without malice,
His fidelity without deceit.
READER, if you would live beloved and die
regretted, profit by the example of DASH.

QUEEN VICTORIA, (1819-1901)

The poor dog, in life the firmest friend,
The first to welcome, foremost to defend.

LORD BYRON, (1788-1824)

CHAPTER 7

DEATH OF A FRIEND

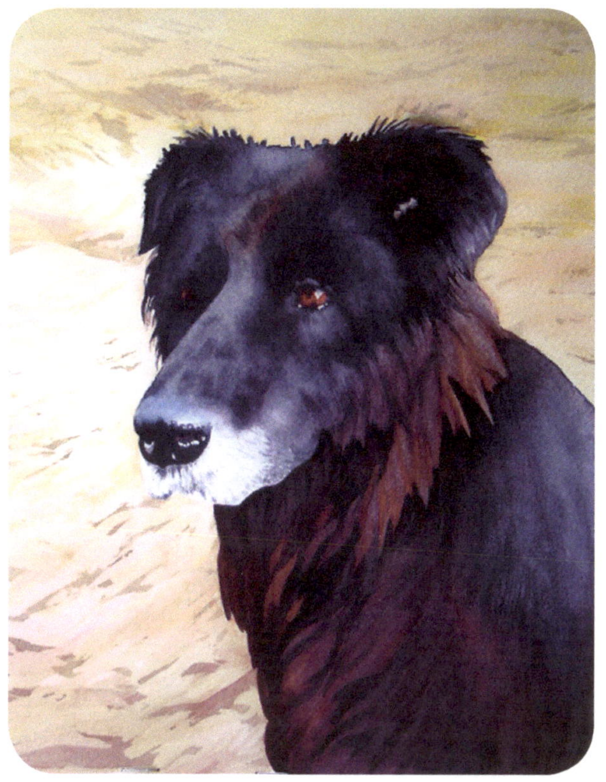

KATHRYN RAGAN

Here Shock, the pride of all his kind, is laid, Who fawned like man, but ne'er like man betrayed.

JOHN GAY, (1685-1732)

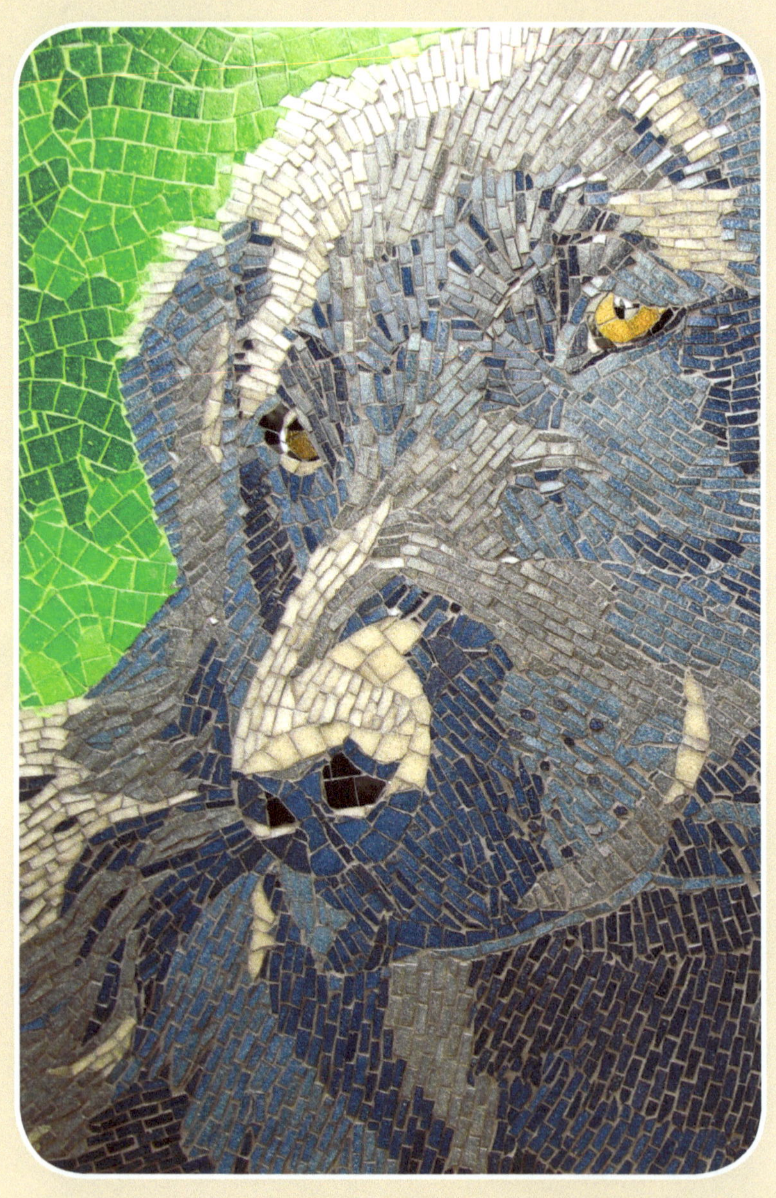

Will Rosie

Chapter 8

Ancient Wisdom

Hurt not animals.

Plutarch, (46-120)

A dog is not considered good because of his barking, and a man is not considered clever because of his ability to talk.

Chuang Tzu, (369-286 B.C.)

The wild boar is often held by a small dog.

Ovid, (43 B.C.-A.D. 17)

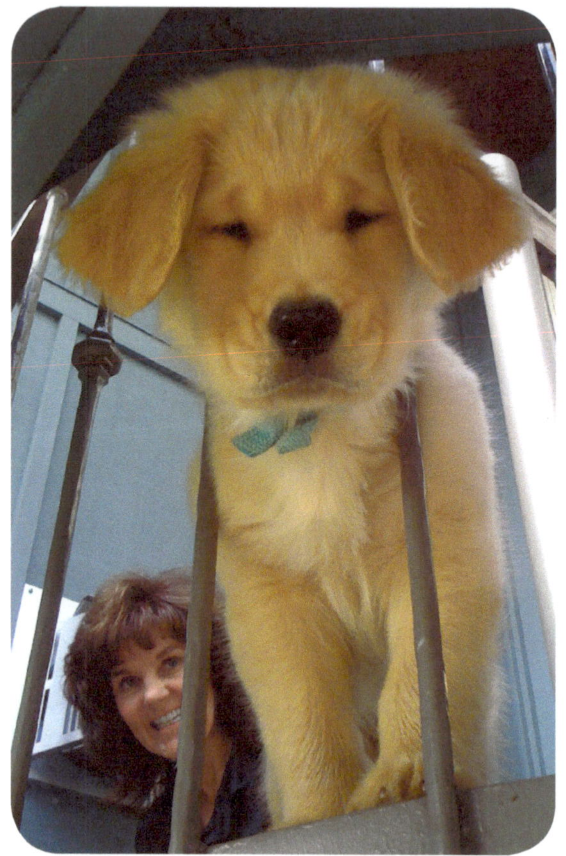

BRAD WHELER

Dogs, according to the old adage, become like their mistresses.

PLATO, (428/427 B.C.-348/347 B.C.)

Thou sayest thou art as weary as a dog,
As angry, sick, and hungry as a dog,
As dull and melancholy as a dog,
As lazy, sleepy, idle as a dog.

But why dost thou compare thee to a dog?
In that for which all men despise a dog,
I will compare thee better to a dog.
Thou are fair and comely as a dog,
Thou are true and honest as a dog,
Thou are kind and liberal as a dog,
Thou are as wise and valiant as a dog.

Sir John Davies, (1569-1626)

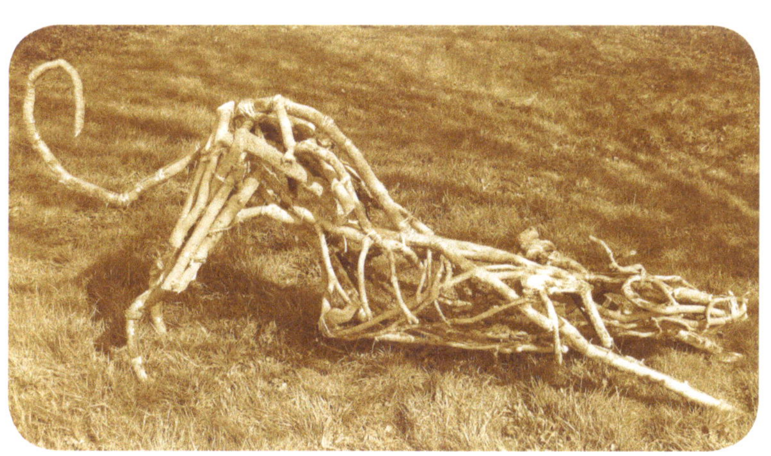

Amanda Hughes

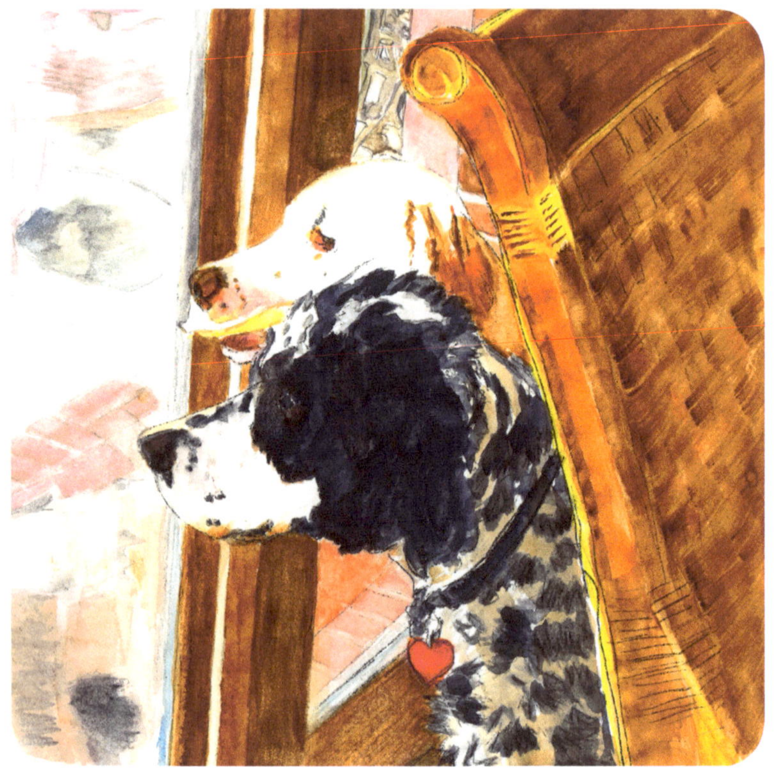

KAREN TRAVIS

The dog teaches thee fidelity

ANTHONY HORNECK, (1641-1697)

Every dog is a lion at home.

GIOVANNI TORRIANO, (C. 1666)

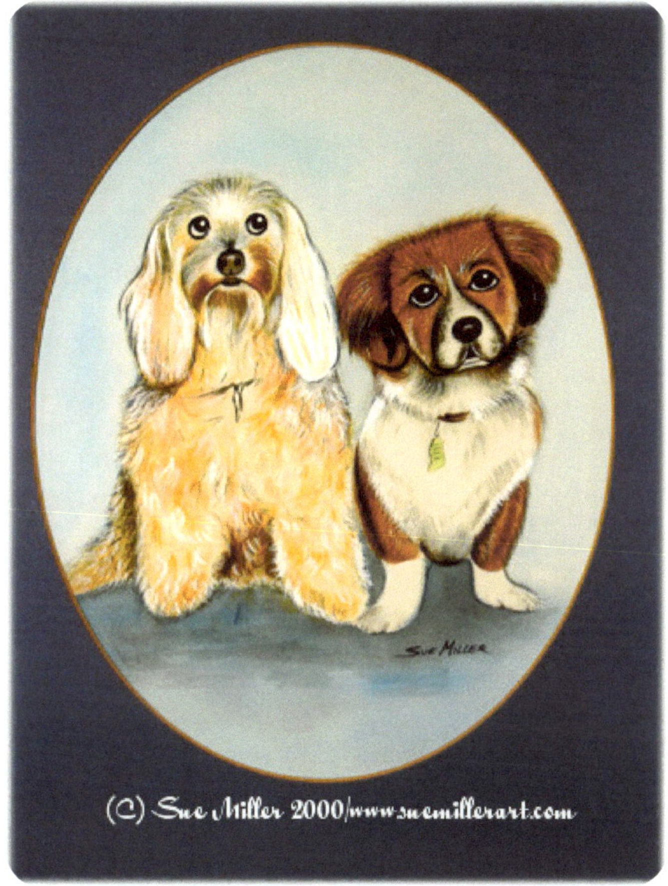

SUE MILLER

Are dogs divided into hes and shes, or do they both share equally in hunting and in keeping watch and in the other duties of dogs?

PLATO, (428/427 B.C.-348/347 B.C.)

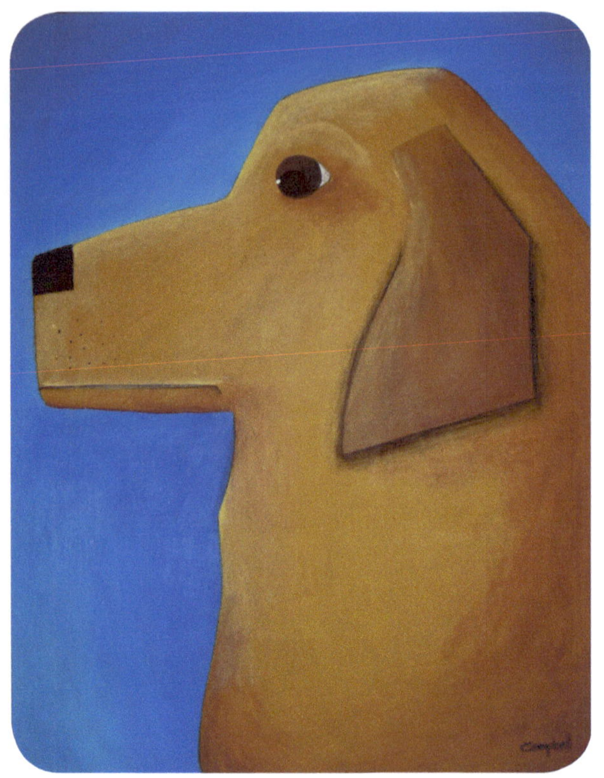

TIM CAMPBELL

Dogs and philosophers do the greatest good and get the fewest rewards.

DIOGENES OF SINOPE (412 B.C.-323 B.C.)

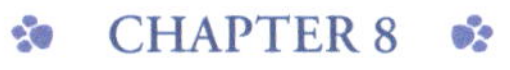

CHAPTER 8

ANCIENT WISDOM

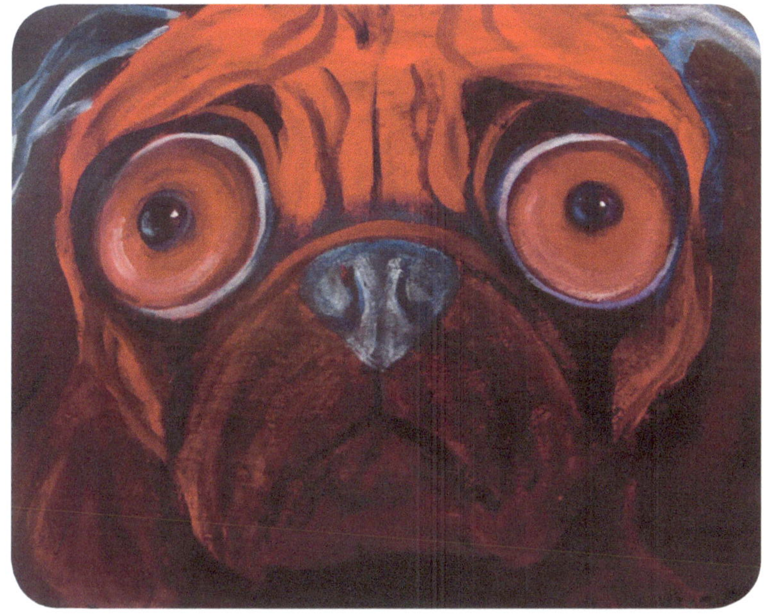

Lynda Mason

He who wishes to kill his dog, accuses him of madness.

Eustache Deschamps, (1346-1406)

Even a dog gets his revenge.

Plutarch, (46-120)

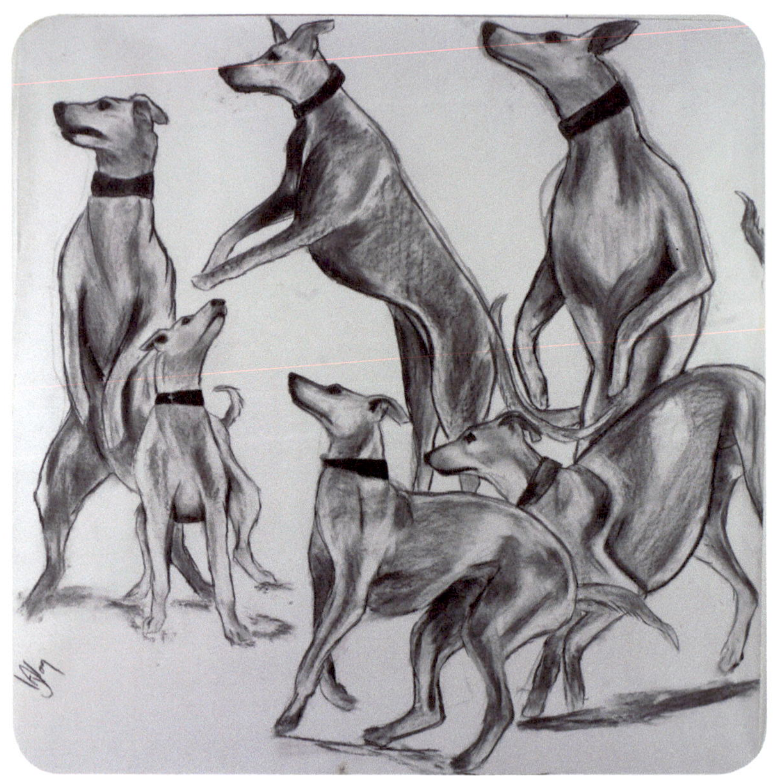

Amanda Hughes

Other persons in selecting a well-bred dog create a circle of flame and place all the pups in the middle of it, and they believe that one to be the best which the mother first runs up to save.

Ulisse Aldrovandi, (1522-1605)

CHAPTER 8

ANCIENT WISDOM

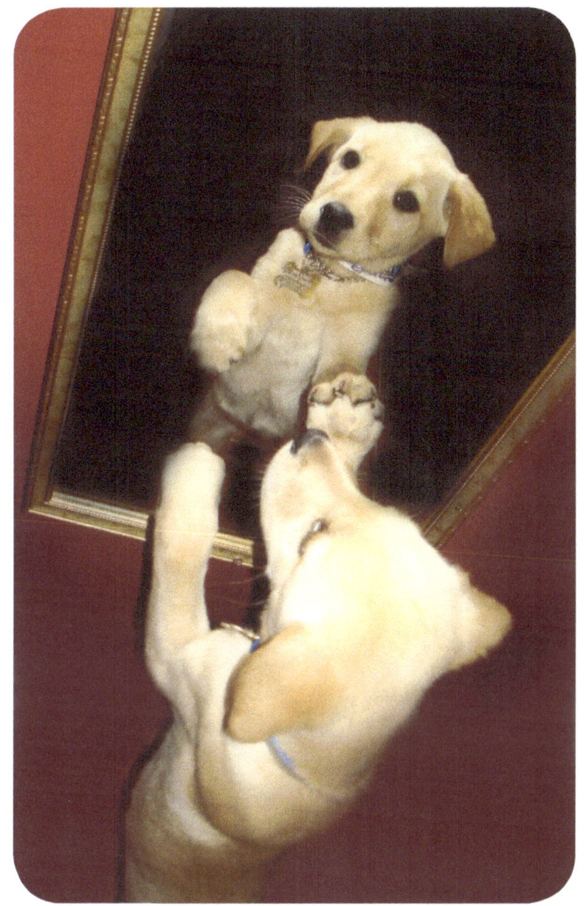

Victoria Patchen

Your dog is your only philosopher.

Plato, (428/427 B.C.-348/347 B.C.)

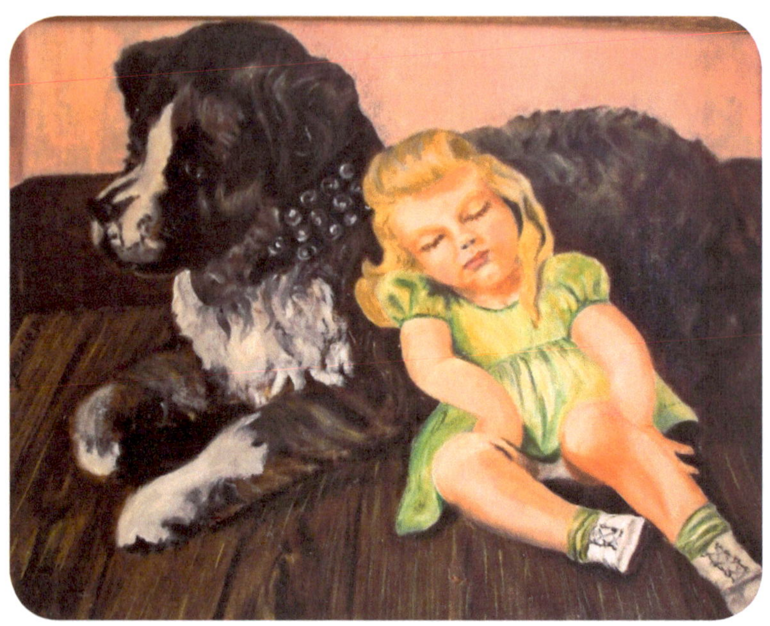

Darle Miller

Nature teaches beasts to know their friends.

William Shakespeare, (1564-1616)

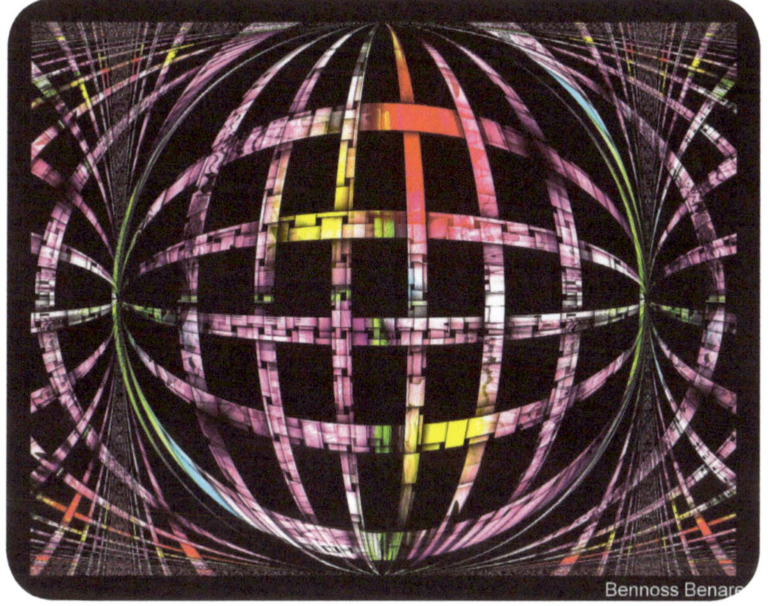

Benjamin Conradi

Your dog is a true philosopher… because he distinguishes the face of a friend and of an enemy only by the criterion of knowing and not knowing. And must not the creature he fond of learning who determines what is friendly and what is unfriendly by the test of knowledge and ignorance?

Plato, (428/427 B.C.-348/347 B.C.)

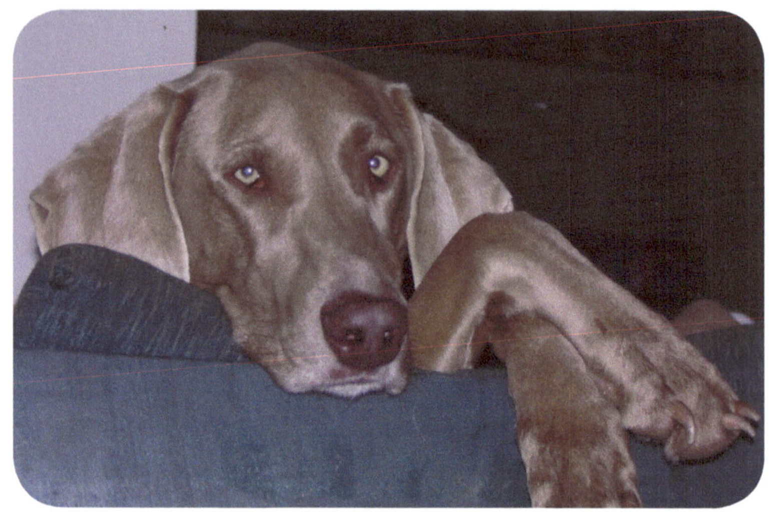

Gene Gissin

A dog hath true love,
A dog have right good understanding,
A wise dog knoweth all things,
A dog hath force and kindliness,
A dog hath mettle and is comely,
A dog is in all things seemly.
A knowing dog thinketh no evil,
A dog hath a memory that forsaketh not,
I say unto you again a dog forsaketh not his duty,
Hath might and cunning therewith and a great
brave heart.

Gace de la Vigne, (c.1300)

CHAPTER 8

ANCIENT WISDOM

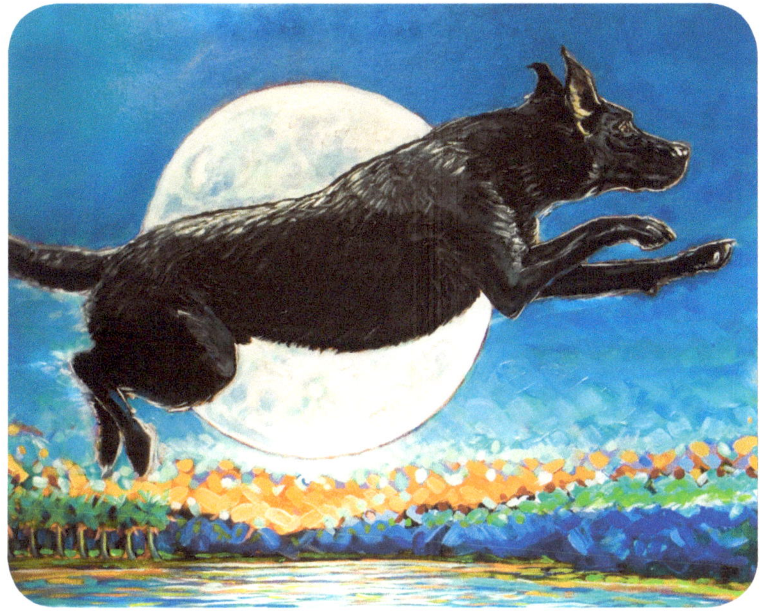

Kevin Rockwell

It is said that dogs drink from the Nile running, lest a crocodile should seize them.

Phaedrus, (15 B.C.-50 A.D.)

Beware of a silent dog and silent water.

William Robson, (c.1585)

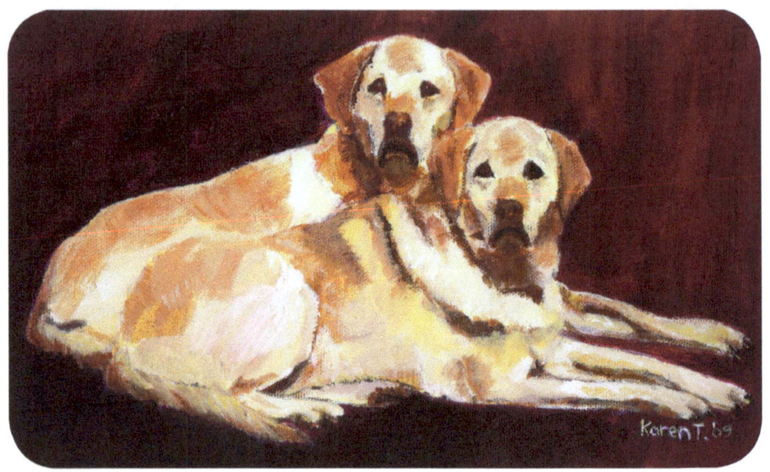

KAREN TRAVIS

I know well enough that there have been dogs so loving that they have thrown themselves into the same grave with the dead bodies of their master; others have stayed upon their masters' graves without stirring a moment from them, and have voluntarily starved themselves to death, refusing to touch the food that was brought them.

MIGUEL DE CERVANTES, (1547-1616)

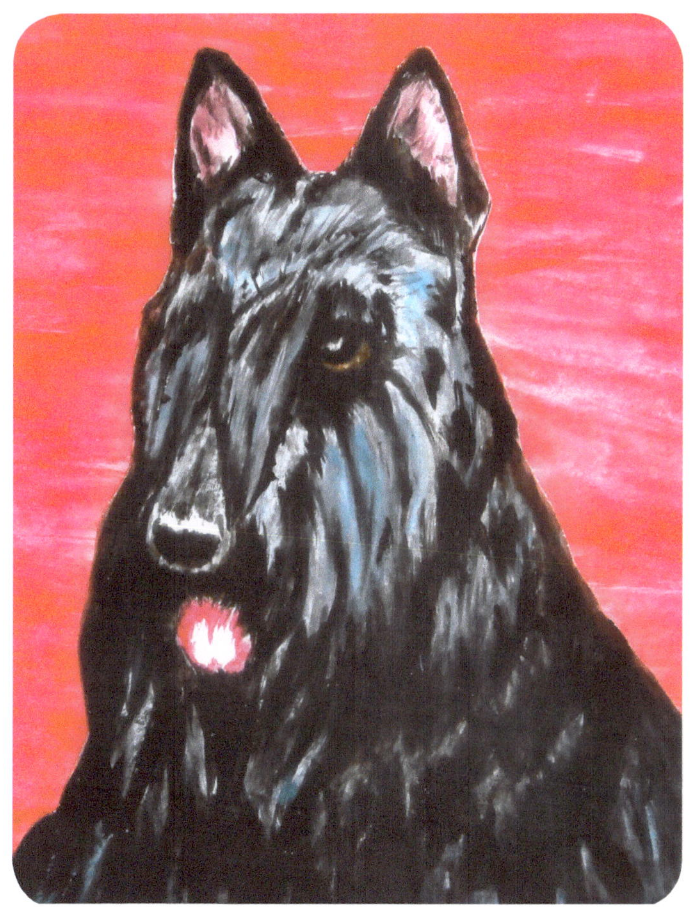

Elena Anfalova

A dog will never forget the crumb thou gavest him.

Sa'di, (1184-1291)

Artists & Photographers Biographies

Elena Anfalova—Page 35, 43, 89, 107

Elena Anfalova is twenty-five and currently resides in Saint-Peterburg, Russia. Anfalova works in both photography and drawing and captures the spirits of animals in both mediums. To date, Anfalova has used colored pencil and acrylic paints for her artworks. Her dog artworks have focused on several breeds, including Dalmatians and Scottish Terriers.

Celia Atkins—Page 34, 39, 45, 84

Celia Atkins is a professional artist who has a home studio near Bishop's Cleeve, Cheltenham, UK. She is currently working in acrylics, oils, pastels and watercolors. Animals are frequently featured in her work and include horses, lions and, of course, numerous breeds of dogs. It is in her pastel portraits that Atkins features four legged friends such as dogs and horses. Celia's website www.atkinsart.co.uk includes more information about her work.

Kerry Ball—Page 10

Based in the Nottinghamshire region of the United Kingdom, Kerry Ball specializes in animal portraits and is also an amateur photographer. In 2009, Ball began her own photography business, Digital Country. Ball is also deeply involved in equestrian events and her work has been featured in All Horses Magazine, Equestrian Life Magazine and Nottinghamshire Today. Work can be viewed and purchased online at www.digitalcountry.webs.com.

Kerri Bisner—Page 33

Hobby photographer Kerri Bisner is currently "dog mother" to a nine-month-old Newfie named Angus. She is a retired investment banker and Wellesley college graduate. Kerri and her husband Michel spend their time between Manchester by the Sea, Massachusetts and their home in Warren, Vermont.

Bennoss Benares (Benjamin Conradi)—Page 103

Benjamin Cocadi is the artist known as Bennoss Benares, creator of TheClimateChangesArt. He was born in Germany in 1972. While drawn to music, and specifically the drums at a young age, he was also drawn to photography in part due to his father's passion for the medium. He can be found on Facebook at TheClimateChangesArt.

Tim Campbell—Page 12, 98

Tim Campbell describes himself as a self-taught/outsider artist. His work can be seen in galleries throughout New England, Cape Cod, Atlanta and San Francisco. Additionally, his art is featured at the American Folk Art Gallery in New York City. His sculptural pieces are created entirely from recycled wood and metal. His painted furniture uses vintage pieces, which gives them their primitive appearance. Each piece is unique and one-of-a-kind. More information about Tim Campbell's work can be found at www.tcampbellart.com.

Kathy Carmichael—Page 40

Lili Chin—Page 16, 62

Lili Chin lives in Los Angeles and does portraits of her own canine companion Boogie, a Boston Terrier. She also works on custom pet portraits for other dog lovers. A passionate dog lover, Chin gives a percentage of all her dog portrait work to Boston Buddies and other organizations that focus on dog rescue. To see more of her dog drawings or to purchase custom pet portraits, please visit www.doggiedrawings.net. When not drawing dogs, Lili Chin designs and produces animated cartoons via www.fwakanimation.com.au.

Katherine Conroy—Page 17

Katherine Conroy is a Massachusetts native who received her BA in Hispanic Studies from Boston College. While at Boston College she took several art classes, but is mostly self-taught. Conroy lived in Southern Spain for four years where she taught English. Now she has returned to the United States and is continuing to focus on her painting and drawing. Additional work can be viewed at www.katherinemconroy.com.

Benjamin Conradi—Page 103

See Bennoss Benares above.

Dylan Cunningham—Page 59

Dylan is a talented and motivated 9-year-old artist who is home schooled. He loves his two dogs, Cody and Goldie and on Fridays looks forward to the art class he attends at his local co-op!

Maria De Leon—Page 71

Maria De Leon is 26 years old and lives in Hillsboro, Oregon. Her hobbies include reading, drawing, and writing poetry. Maria's photographs feature her two-year-old dog Koda, who is also her best friend. You can find out more information about this artist at www.facebook.com/Maria.deleon.13 and www.facebook.com/Maria.deleon.13.

Patricia Denys—Page 65

Patricia Denys graduated with a BFA from the University of Texas at Austin and received her MFA at Vermont College. Recently, Denys has presented papers at the School of Visual Arts Conference on how society views both animals and women. Her work has been published in the SVA's "Proceedings." Denys latest work centers on exposing the dichotomies between society's perception of how animals raised for human consumption are treated and the reality of how these animals are, in fact, treated. You can learn more about Patricia Denys at www.schoolofvisualarts.edu/ug/index.jsp?sid0=1&sid1=46&page_id=497.

KYLIE FARRELLY—PAGE 67

Kylie Farrelly resides in Newstead, Queensland and holds a Bachelor of Education degree from Queensland University of Technology. She is an art teacher and tutor. In 2004, she had her first solo art exhibition. To date, she has held seven solo exhibitions. Further, her work has been in thirteen additional group exhibitions. Farrellys has had numerous private commissions and currently enjoys gallery representation from Gallery 2120 in Brisbane, Australia. More about this artist can be found at www.kyliefarrelly.com.au.

CANDACE FENANDER—PAGE 42

Candace Fenander is an artist living in Hawaii who is producing vibrant works using acrylics and oils. Candace has attended numerous pastel workshops and draws inspiration form watercolorist such as Roger Whitlock. She is also a member of the Pastel Artists of Hawaii and serves as the organizations Webmaster, showchair and newsletter editor. For more of her work visit candacefenander.com.

JESSICA GALVIN—PAGE 32, 51

SUSAN GERTZ—PAGE 87

Artist Susan Gertz has worked as a collage artist for over 20 years. Her love of animals and her appreciate of the role that they play in people's lives manifested itself with the founding of Dogpatch Pix. This company offers unique and stunning portrait photos of pets as well as custom digital collages. Currently, she lives with her husband and three dog companions, Darwin, Garrison and Gus. View more of Gertz's work at www.dogpatchpix.com.

Gene Gissin—Page 11, 21, 104

Gene Gissin is a graduate of RIT College of Graphic Arts and Photography. He owns Gene Gissin Photography where he specializes in photographing everything from weddings to pets. Further, Gissin also works in photojournalism and has taught photography at Cazenovia College in New York. Today, he is the President of the Professional Photographers Society of Central New York. For more of Gissin's work, visit his website at www.gissinphoto.com.

Robby Glass—Page 66

Robby is a Cazenovia native and a student at St. Lawrence University. Photography is one of his many interests, which also includes sailing, writing, travel, water skiing, and downhill skiing. He has a passion for helping others through service and philanthropy. Robby is a life long dog lover.

Evelyn Grant—Page 74

Evelyn Grant is a thirty-two year old mother of four who grew up with a love of art and design. She is currently exploring her passion for art via graphic design. Through her work, Grant strives to capture the majesty and complexity of the Boxer breed.

Abby Gregory—Page 37, 50

Abby Gregory was born to British parents in Switzerland in 1979. In 1989, she moved to Cheltenham, England. Animals have always fascinated her. When Abby's passion for photography developed, it was only natural for her to seek to capture photographs of animals. In May 2010, she achieved the distinction of a Canine Psychology Diploma. She currently volunteers for Cheltenham Animal Shelter, which can be visited at www.gawa.org.uk.

Anja Hammefahr—Page 77

More about Anja's work can be found at www.crisushand friends.de.

Kari Shay Henning—Page 31

Kari Shay Henning is an amateur photographer residing in Lincoln, Nebraska. In the fall of 1994, Kari participated in the Lifetouch competition where she was 1st runner up in the Mountain/Plains region. More of her work can be viewed at www.karishaypics.ifp3.com.

Jean Hildebrant—Page 64, 79

As a child, Jean Hildebrant was drawn to art. She worked with oil and pastel mediums and specialized in figurative works and portraits. Later, Hildebrant began attending workshops and eventually won scholarships to the Scottsdale Artists School. Her work has received numerous awards and can be found in various corporate, private and public collections. Hildebrant is a charter member of the Pastel Society of Oregon. More information can be found at www.JeanHildebrant.com.

Amanda Hughes—Page 20, 29, 95, 100

Currently based in Kent, United Kingdom, Amanda Hughes is nearing completion of her BA in Fine Arts from the University of Kent. A devoted dog lover, Hughes has been drawing and painting dogs for years. She is currently enjoying sharing her vibrant and detailed work with the public.

Jay Jude—Page 76

Jay has been interested in photography his whole life. You can see more of Jay's work at www.jaynjude.deviantart.com.

Kary Kidder—Page 54, 55

Kary Kidder is a passionate dog lover from Covington, Washington. She is the caregiver of no less than six pugs, three of which are rescue dogs. Kidder has quite literally raised a small zoo of animals, ranging from chickens and rabbits to hermit crabs, donkeys, snakes and lizards. She is also the owner of www.onesmugpug.com, a site dedicated to commission portraits of pugs. Kary also sells her art at www.zazzle.com/karykid. Recently, Kidder has won several awards for her oil paintings and is now working in photography.

Yvonne Lautenschlager—Page 61

Yvonne Lautenschlager is a Hamburg, Germany based artist. She has a medical degree and has worked in Orthopedic Medicine as well as Chinese Medicine. She is married with an eighteen-year-old son, a dog and two cats. Yvonne is very active creating new art, writing and maintaining her blog. To see more of Yvonne's work, visit medeasspace.blogspot.com.

Perry Lindh—Page 78

Perry Lindh lives in Canberra, Australia where she lives with her three dogs Fifi, Fonzi and Boris, her cat Flanders, two parrots, three aviaries full of canaries as well as finches, parrots and a cockatoo! Fifi and Fonzi have an active social life, as they are engaged to be married. They accompany Lindh each and every day to the grooming salon that she owns.

Gill Low—Page 86

Gill Low is a professional artist who currently lives and works in Fife in Scotland. When she was only 9 years old, her mother sent her to painting classes. She has been drawing and painting all her life. Gill Low focuses primarily on pet portraits, but her work also has been highly influenced by the Scottish landscape. She is currently involved in various workshops and demonstrations. More information about Gill Low can be found at www.thedam.org.uk/artists/gill_low.php and orrville.weebly.com.

Lynda Mason—Page 99

Lynda Mason has a passion for animal art of all sorts including impressive, detailed and imaginative equine art. In fact, Mason is quick to point out that the main focus of her art is in some fashion involves horses or animals in general. One of her primary goals in her paintings is to have viewers see the world through the perspective of another species. Lynda Mason's conceptual animal art and equine portraiture can be viewed at www.horseofadifferentcolorart.com.

Mary McAndrews—Page 72

Mary McAndrews holds a BA in Art from Buffalo State and has also studied art at the Academy of Realistic Art in Toronto, Canada. To date, McAndrew's work has including illustration for Nature Centers as well as CD album cover art and book cover art. Additionally, McAndrew worked as Director of the Museum of European Art in Clarence, New York. More information about this artist can be found at www.marymcandrew.com as well as her online store www.zazzle.com/marymcandrew.

Kerry McGuire—Page 26,27

Kerry states, "Irish Wolfhounds have a hold of my heart and soul." It was the loss of her hound, Minute, to bone cancer at 5 years of age, that sent her on the journey to sketching. Previously, she had been making her living mostly as a sculptor through her business, Gar-den-Goyles where she designed and cast concrete garden art, wholesale to nurseries and specialty garden stores. Her work can be scene at "Art of the Wolfhound" on facebook.

Darle Miller—Page 102

Darle has been painting for pleasure for over 60 years. The painting titled My Donna with her dog Pal on page 102 was completed in the 1960's. She is an animal lover who lives in Watertown, NY.

Sue Miller—Page 8, 97

Artist Sue Miller began painting at a young age and attended the University of Massachusetts where she studied fine arts. Further, Miller received private art lessons from such renowned painters as Rachel Farrington and Milton Healey. For twenty years, Miller worked as a professional graphic artist in advertising agencies and newspaper art departments. She also founded The Magic Palette Art Studio, which has taught thousands of students both painting and drawing over the past fifteen years. Additional information about this artist's work can be found at www.suemillerart.com.

Sue Caroline Ogden—Page 83

Artist Sue Odgen is a Provincetown, MA resident who lives in a community rich with artists and writers. Odgen has dedicated her live to her love and appreciation of animals and worked for a whale watching company for twenty-eight years. Her dog Tex, who is a combination beagle/basset mix, (also known as a "Bagel") is the subject of a book called the "Tex Text Book."

Victoria Patchen—Page 28, 30, 101

Victoria Patchen lives in the DC area with her husband, 3 rescue cats, and 1 rescue dog. She volunteers with Lucky Dog Animal Rescue in DC. In fact, Victoria started taking photos of her foster dogs in order to help market them to potential adopters. She is also a singer/songwriter, writes & performs with The District All-Stars (electro-pop, Facebook.com/TheDistrictAllStars) and Lucky Day (pop/rock Facebook.com/LuckyDayBand). To find out more about her solo work, visit Facebook.com/VictoriaPatchen. Additional information about Victoria's pet photos can be found at Facebook.com/VictoriaPatchenPhotography.

RACHEL PARKER—PAGE 14, 36, 38, 46, 75

Rachel Parker began painting in 2000 and is self-taught. However, Parker has been drawing since she was a child. She is currently working primarily in watercolor and animals are among her favorites subjects. "Dramatic lighting can make a potato sack beautiful. Light is a life-giving force, and this is true in a painting as well—it breathes vitality and a sense of awe into the every day," says Rachel. Prints of Rachel's work and links to her Facebook group are available on www.rachelsstudio.com. She also has a blog at www.rachelsstudio.blogspot.com.

JESSICA PELSUE—PAGE 13

Jessica Pelsue is a native New Englander from Massachusetts and has a keen passion for travel, photography and, of course, her dog. During her travels, she frequently documents their journeys in the form of photos.

KATHRYN RAGAN—PAGE 48, 91

Kathryn Ragan produces her paintings from a small farm outside of beautiful Vancouver, British Columbia. For the last ten years, Ragan, a self-taught artist, has worked in watercolor due to her love of the medium's "transparency, fluidity and unpredictability." Recently, Ragan was accepted into the International Guild of Realism. See more of her work at www.studioatthefarm.ca.

Kevin W. Rockwell—Page 18, 24, 58, 68, 105

Kevin W. Rockwell graduated from the Ringling College of Art and Design in 1980 with a focus in illustration and design. He has worked as a medical illustrator for the Medical University of South Carolina. Rockwell is currently active in different pet focused charitable organizations, such as the Pet Helpers pet shelter in Charleston, South Carolina. For the last ten years, Rockwell has been painting pets and dogs. More than 70 paintings can be viewed online at his site www.RockwellArts.com.

Will Rosie—Page 92

Will Rosie lives with his wife and three children in Southampton, United Kingdom. One of Rosie's artistic passions is working with mosaics and creating impression mosaic designs. Rosie feels that mosaics are simultaneously beautiful and communicative and have a unique place in history. Additional information about this artist and his exquisite, hand-crafted, bespoke mosaics can be found at www.sublimemosaics.info.com.

Donna Rosser—Page 44, 60, 80

Throughout her career, fine art photographer Donna Rosser has had her work featured in numerous magazines and newspapers. More recently, Rosser has transitioned to digital photography and has developed a love for black and white imagery. Her work is becoming increasingly digital in its focus, and she is using her laptop as her darkroom. Rosser's love of dogs merges with her passion for photography. In the process, her award-winning work has been created. Visit Rosser's blog at thebarefootphotographer.blogspot.com.

Charles Thompson—Page 23

Charles Thompson is a performance consultant who resides in Greenville, South Carolina with his wife LaVerne, feline companions Zoom and Betty Grable and their canine friend Callie. Thompson enjoys the great outdoors and spends much of his free time scuba diving, hiking and photographing nature.

Karen Travis—Page 88, 96, 106

Karen Travis lives in Park City, Utah, where she is able to use the beauty of nature for inspiration. Travis has enjoyed a love of painting for as long as she can remember. She received her Masters in Illustration from Syracuse University in New York State. Travis draws heavily on her own life experiences for inspiration in creating her work. She hopes to allow others to feel part of the joy she has discovered within the creative process. More of her art can be viewed at kaleidascopedesigns.com.

William Travis—Page 57, 63

Bill Travis is a life-long dog owner and lover who fully believes that the domesticated dog is man's best invention to date. Are there any creatures more loving and dedicated than dogs? Travis lives in an 1850's converted stone church near Leesburg, Virginia. He has three dogs: two Jack Russell Terriers named Tyler and BB; and a Chihuahua mix named Shadow. They run the show at Newvalley Church and are always ready to play, eat, and give mass quantities of love. Make room in your heart! Please adopt.

Pamela Utton—Page 53, 70, 73

Residing in Baker, Florida, Pam Utton is a self-taught artist who has emerged her love of animals and art. In fact, it was her love of animals that inspired her to paint. Today, Utton is frequently called upon to paint pets from around the world. She is also an avid photographer and home designer. Her websites include pamutton.blogspot.com and two online stores www.etsy.com/shop/petportraitart and www.zazzle.com/pamutton.

Gabrielle Utz—Page 15, 41, 47, 52

Gabrielle Utz specializes in high-quality murals. In particular, she is recognized as one of the leading muralists in what is called the "European Old Master Style." Many of her works have been publicly acclaimed as masterpieces. Further, Utz has a very precise view of art and the emotions that it should invoke stating, "Art should make you feel better. It should communicate to you." To view more of her work, you can visit three websites www.artcomm.us, www.boysandgirlsmurals.com and www.artstudio88.com.

Cynthia Van Savage—Page 56

Cynthia Van Savage is the founder of The Clyde Fund and Clyde's Sanctuary. Clyde was named after a very special homeless German Shepherd that Van Savage adopted. Clyde had a profound impact on Van Savage's life for a variety of reasons, one of which was that Clyde charmingly barked whenever Van Savage played the piano. Today, Van Savage helps promote the importance of animals in people's lives through The Clyde Fund. To learn more about Van Savage and Clyde visit www.clydemania.com.

Brad Wheler—Page 94

See About the Author on page 131.

Valarie Wolf—Page 19, 82

Valarie Wolf is an artist who resides in Orange County, California where she lives with her husband and two energetic Italian Greyhouses. Wolf is also a member of the American Academy of Equine Art. Valarie's is passionate about animals in general and donates part of the proceeds of her paintings to various animal welfare groups. Learn more about Valarie and her art at www.valariewolf.com.

Index of Quotations

About the Author

BRADFORD G. WHELER is the former CEO, President and Co-owner of Allan Electric Company. He sold the company to a New York Stock Exchange listed company back when the stock market was hot. After staying on as President during the transition period, Brad retired.

Brad's lifelong love of history, art, books and the inherent humor in man's nature lead to the founding of BookCollaborative.com, and the publishing of this book as well as "SNAPPY SAYINGS; wit & wisdom from the world's greatest minds".

Brad's various community involvements include being Chairman of the Board of Trustees of Cazenovia College, a member of the Board of Directors of the Greater Cazenovia Area Chamber of Commerce, Chairman of the Board of Directors and Alumni Association and President of the Sigma Phi Society at Cornell University in Ithaca, NY.

Brad holds a BS and ME in Civil and Environmental Engineering from Cornell University in Ithaca, NY as well as a MBA degree from Fordham University in New York, NY, Additionally, he is a Licensed Professional Engineer in New York and several other states. He is also a graduate of the Manlius Pebble Hill School. Brad his wife Julie and their golden retriever Quincy live in Cazenovia, NY.

www.ingramcontent.com/pod-product-compliance
Lightning Source LLC
LaVergne TN
LVHW052253100826
845147LV00001B/26
* 9 7 8 0 9 8 2 2 5 3 8 2 3 *